Gestures of the Heart

Gestures of the Heart

*A Guide for Healing the
Residue of Life's Traumas:
Songs of Manifestation*

Second Edition

Pamela V. Church

GESTURES OF THE HEART

The information in this book is not intended to replace or substitute for the medical advice of physicians or other qualified health care providers. Rather, it is intended to help readers maximize the benefits of that advice and achieve an ever greater depth of well-being.

Interior illustrations by Cary Porter
Cover illustration by Karl Pilato
Cover design by Patte Lazarus

ISBN-10:   0-9795101-0-4
ISBN-13:   978-0-9795101-0-6
Printed in the United States of America on acid-free paper
9   8   7   6   5   4   3   2

Dedication

With deep thanks and love to Bud, Susan, and Miles.
With gratitude to Catherine Harold, the original publisher,
for her vision and open heart.

May any merit from this work
be dedicated to the healing of all beings.

Contents

Part IV. Addendum for Clinicians

Related Resources

Index

Part I.

Befriending the Body,

Opening the Vision

1.

For Us All:

Healing the Residue of Trauma

I believe that we all want harmony, to live in harmony in the world community, in our families, to have harmony in our bodies. This book is about being on that dusty road we all travel hoping to find happiness, looking for freedom. Big elusive words, and yet we can't shake them. We keep coming back to them knowing they are important but sometimes not knowing quite how to realize them.

In our culture today, the first decade of the 21st century, many of us suffer from what I am calling *trauma residue syndrome.* It's about living in a stressful, largely urban culture cut off from our inner resources, doing the best we can to get by day to day, and yet feeling diminished, perhaps demoralized, not all here. There could be a low-grade background depression that seems to go on forever. There could be a loss of a job, loss of a loved one, a disruptive life change that we can't quite seem to spring back from, various events that seem to drain life energy. Or we could have had abuse in our life experience, gone to therapy, done our work, and still the sky is gray. This or that, the bottom line is about not living our full potential.

Most everyone has heard of post-traumatic stress disorder (PTSD). Originally it was used to describe what happened to soldiers devastated from the effects of war. Now the diagnosis has been enlarged to include experiences where a person feels overwhelmed with fear, horror, or helplessness. Unlike PTSD, trauma residue syndrome is not a label of pathology to be included in the *Diagnostic & Statistical Manual of Mental Disorders*. It is my description of how difficult it is to live in a highly technological, fast-paced society with any kind of sustained well-being. It is a description of the previous hurts that interfere with life in the here and now. It is a description of our shared humanity as we each try to do our best day to day and often find it daunting.

Trauma residue syndrome is what I believe most of us inhabit if only by way of living complex lives full of stress and strain. We sweep the kitchen regularly, but do we clear and balance the nervous system regularly, so that we can have full resource? In our busy lives, it is difficult to take time and feel our feelings. What's the point, you ask, since so many feelings are uncomfortable anyway? If the feelings aren't consciously felt and experienced, they get wired into the background noise of our nervous system. They don't go away; they go underground. For example, you may find yourself getting upset and a moment later realize that the upset is mostly about something else that happened at a different time. These feelings want to wash through but need a vehicle to do so.

What if our resource for healing the effects of trauma residue syndrome was close at home, just waiting to be utilized? What if the resource was our body, plain and simple? What if we could decode the language of our symptoms, our aches and pains, our hunches, our hopes? What if we could metabolize what is going on in the moment, so that our bodies would be free to move forward unburdened by the past?

Happiness and harmony are some of our greatest resources. In this book, you'll find energy protocols that help maximize those resources. The energy protocols are experiential tools to work with feeling states and stored body sensations, so that the body's wisdom and peace can come forward. A simple way to be in the body and heal. A simple way to focus heart, mind, and body on an intention and bring that intention forward. And with only an occasional exception, each of the protocols takes less than 10 minutes to do.

My experience is that if we can be fully with what is going on in the moment, whatever is going on in the moment, then what happens is that the feeling biochemically releases from our cells, awaiting the next moment. This gives us the opportunity to be in the present moment unencumbered by holding back or jumping to the future. Does this sound like a take on ideas thousands of years old? You bet. What I bring here is a new adaptation, a new therapeutic use, for those age-old, wisdom-filled ideas in a growing area of work known as energy psychology or energy medicine.

Energy Medicine

I am keenly interested in energy medicine personally and professionally. My background is clinical psychology. I have been in private practice since 1980 seeing individuals, couples, adolescents, and families. For much of that time I have facilitated groups in the schools and in the community at large. I have a general practice, and yet the people who come to see me for the most part have some kind of trauma that they are working through. It is astounding how many of us are carrying wounds from harm done to us emotionally, physically, or sexually. Despite all wishes, these wounds don't heal on their own.

The dilemma is that it can take a long time to recover, and that it is both expensive and time consuming. So several of us decided to help others begin the healing process as early as possible, and we developed a program called Chrysalis for middle schools and high schools. We got a grant and did groups for boys and girls who had been abused. Much gratitude was expressed by the kids, who got information about some of the painful effects of abuse, got to share feelings with others who had similar experiences, and learned new coping skills. Okay, good stuff, but the grant did eventually run out. Now what?

I began to explore some of the trainings around energy psychology that were geared toward clinicians. A wonderful part of this is that we got to learn these new techniques by practicing on ourselves. To that point, I had been in therapy on and off for years. In my field, one can't begin to help facilitate someone else's healing until we have some measure of our own healing. I was amazed at the depth and quickness of change that I felt in myself when doing energy work. So I studied more, found a therapist who was skilled in these various techniques, and got to work.

Some of the techniques I liked, some I was not as fond of. I experimented with the techniques, integrated the ones that worked for me in my daily life, and used them with clients. The deal about energy medicine is that by and large it is incisively effective. It is the body's language to respond to a feeling state with some kind of physical gesture.

One of my skills in the world is synthesizing knowledge and experience, and I began to do that with this new energy medicine. Spontaneously, in my office, I would suggest that a client put one energy technique together with another technique to help access a sensation, ease a feeling, stabilize an intent. Over time, as clients told me about the effects these techniques had, it became clear to me that certain energy techniques were most helpful when placed together into multi-step protocols.

There is such pleasure and mastery in being upset, doing an energy protocol, and then, in less then 10 minutes' time, feeling relief. The protocols work. Clients began doing them outside of their time with me. I did them for myself because I felt increasing clarity the more I integrated them into my daily life. The protocols, energy work in general, provide a hands-on approach to mediate stress and distress. This creates an empowerment that furthers creativity and spontaneity.

One of the blessings of energy medicine is that it is discernible. After doing a protocol or some other energy procedure, a person feels better. Nothing subtle here. There is usually a distinctive increase in a feeling of well-being. You can take an inventory of your level of stress before doing a protocol or some other energy procedure (10 being high distress, 0 being no distress) and then check in with the inventory immediately after the protocol. The protocols are effective, and the body notes the difference.

My influences are many. I am excited about neurobiology and working with the brain. I have formally studied oriental medicine. I am impressed with Brain Gym. I like the contact with Jin Shin acupressure. I have worked with trauma clinically for years and years. I believe it is the heart that heals. Working with the chakras is irrefutably powerful. Combine all of the above, in addition to my experience being on this planet, and you have my voice, my take on things. From this place, I developed the gestures, honed the intent from a physiological perspective, and created the protocols.

What is distinctive about energy medicine is that it does not let us externalize our wisdom. Nobody outside of us knows what is best for our body. The protocols, like other energy medicine, process what is in the body at the moment. By metabolizing the distress, the body can then settle into a deeper knowing that connects feelings with thoughts and insights. Sometimes, it might be a greater calm with nothing added.

One of the places I feel we need to collectively develop more resource is in times of disaster. If the body can be responded to in a moment of shock, it quickens the healing of the heart. Disasters, natural or otherwise, are by definition awful. We can mitigate some of that intensity by doing emotional first aid in the moment. What that looks like is having emergency services trained in energy medicine, and also using what we know for ourselves in a place where we are overwhelmed. Self-soothing when we need it the most. Another needed step might be to add energy medicine in the schools as part of the health curriculum.

The Neurologic Link

There is a belief among many health professionals that, to change, we need to change how we think. This is an important piece, but perhaps overrated. Cognitively changing how we think may bypass the body; then we are back to that old mind/body split. We need to get everything on board to have a profound effect. Mind, body, heart. When we are in a situation of distress, our body is quite activated, in arousal mode, or perhaps we are numb, which can paradoxically be a more intense place. We are so overwhelmed by what we are feeling that we go over the top and pretend we aren't feeling anything.

Neuroscientists are finding that the brain is plastic, that is, capable of change. Neurons are the nerve cells of the nervous system. Their job is two-fold: excitability and conductivity, receiving a signal and sending it. As we learn we develop new synaptic connections between neurons. A myelin sheath coats the axon of the nerve and helps it to conduct nerve impulses. The more the axon is used, the more effective it becomes. Sharon Promislow says that one of the values of myelination is in reinforcing long-term memory. In other words, it helps hard-wire our experience into our nervous system.

What we have as common knowledge is that if we are relaxed, we tend to function more effectively in our lives; if we are tense and pre-occupied, we tend to function more on automatic with less resource available. The energy protocols described in this book help the body to settle in, while keeping in mind a particular issue that might have a charge. This creates new cellular information. The more often the protocol is done, the more enduring the new cellular information becomes.

On a basic level, this idea is neither new nor revolutionary. Dr. John Thie, who developed a holistic approach to restoring natural energy called Touch for Health, says that when we change how we feel, our body chemistry changes. He addressed this issue in the mid 1980s. Dr. Herbert Benson, a Harvard cardiologist, in the mid 1970s articulated what he called the *relaxation response* as a way to lower blood pressure and reduce heart rate. More recently, Candace Pert, in a book called *Molecules of Emotion,* demonstrated how influential our emotions are on all parts of body systems. The research at this point is strong and clear: Emotions effect brain and body chemistry. By changing our emotions, we alter the physiological well-being of the body.

Including the Body

So how then to get back to the body in a kind, safe way. This is what the energy protocols in this book aim for: connections with feelings, with body sensations, in order to lower the heightened state. From this place, our innate wisdom and insight can be accessed.

This creates a new gestalt by having a place of upset, regulating it, becoming more connected to our body, and then tuning into our innate wisdom once the choppy water has settled. The wisdom might be about breathing more deeply, or dropping fear around what we are feeling, or noting a recent accomplishment with pride. It could be anything. We'll know. This kind of listening-in is available to us all. For many people, this is part of what happens in a therapy hour. For sure, and it is not limited to good therapy. This is about building a repertoire of resources. The protocols are ways to take care of ourselves while we are in the midst of everyday life, or in crisis, or consciously working through old patterns that interfere with our being present. Over and over again returning to that true state: our body sensations and feelings in the moment. This time returning with means to help lower the edge of distress, so that we can be with what is wanting our attention. Often the heart is ready to respond; it just needs our initial attention.

Our culture is both obsessed with the body while simultaneously ignoring what is going on in the body. We do this by being disconnected from our feelings. Of course there are many manifestations of this: feeling for others but not for ourselves, putting our feelings into material possessions, feeling only a narrow range of feelings because of previous trauma, putting our feelings into stress-related body symptoms, and on and on.

One way to define body coherence is a felt sensation of being in our body, open to feelings, and receptive to our intuition and insight. When this happens we have the power of being embodied. Joining all three resources—head, heart, and body—gives us the opportunity to be grounded and open, alert and relaxed, ready to meet the day. The protocols can help.

The Effect of Gesture

My understanding of the effects of trauma changed with Alan Schore's work on the right hemisphere and trauma. Trauma—and early trauma—alters the functioning of the brain. The right hemisphere of the brain is the relational side, the hemisphere that is feeling-oriented, both with our joys and our troubles. The bottom line with all the research on neurobiology and brain functioning is that to have full resource we need to make sure the right and left hemispheres are talking to each other. To that end, it's helpful to key into different functions of the brain by touching the areas closest to them.

For example, placing a hand on the forehead sends blood to the prefrontal cortex, which is vital in executive decisions and planning. Placing a hand on the back of the head at the brain stem calms the part of the brain that is geared towards the fight/flight/freeze response. Placing one hand on the forehead and one hand at the brain stem connects with the neuralvascular points at the prefrontal cortex, which can help influence what feels like the most rational thing to do, for instance in a moment of terror. I call this gesture *Brain Flow Mudra.* It is similar to what neurologists call frontal-occipital holding. For *Brain Flow Mudra,* the intent is to make contact with the hind brain, which is sometimes called the lizard brain, bridging the occiput with the brain stem. The brain stem is key here. It is a major player in the language of energy gestures, as you will see later in this book.

In my experience, combining an intention with a physical gesture such as what I've just described exponentially increases the potency of the intention. We all have experience of naming a goal for ourselves, an intent, following through, and feeling much satisfaction. This aligning with an intent and following through can be one of the deeper pleasures of life. The protocols in this book are designed with a particular intent that is paired with physical gestures that tap into the body's energy centers—such as chakras and acupuncture meridians, which are described in more detail in the next chapter.

The two together, intent and physical gesture, send a focused signal to the nervous system. The nervous system is often relieved to get such a clear signal and will do what it can to accommodate the signal. In the experience of the body, what this can mean is relief from distress and access to greater perception. This way of working with the body, I am calling *somatically accessed wisdom.*

There is no other place to start but with the immediate experience in the body in this moment. This is the beginning, the middle, and the end. We feel whatever sensations are there, pleasant or unpleasant, note them with awareness, and proceed from there. These body sensations are the way in. The problem is that they could be habitual responses to stress and there could be a lot of static associated with them. Most of us have conditioned responses in our body that we automatically go to when under duress. Some of us get headaches, others of us get stomachaches, or we become prone to accidents. The variations are endless. You know your story. Now we get to notice them, be curious what is underneath them, and what they are trying to tell us that we are not quite hearing. If we got it, they would appear less often.

The Hero's Journey

All cultures further certain characteristics and ignore others. At a certain point, the underdeveloped characteristics may come around and assert themselves. The culture at large may be skeptical and fascinated with these split off qualities. Notice, in our culture, the resurgence of heroes with extraordinarily honed intuition and intent, physical dedication paired with an earned-as-they-go integrity like Frodo and Samwise in *Lord of the Rings.* Young ones who rise to the occasion with valor despite formidable obstacles. Popular culture can produce these moving snapshots of what we have left behind and what we are to bring forward to regenerate in a vital way. It may be time to bring forward the hero's wholeness, knowing that the hero's journey begins with a regular person, no one special. The hero archetype asks us to use all of our resource to be here now, to open to our full possibility.

For many, the hero's journey has been transforming hardship and trauma through 12-step programs, therapy, body work. We need support to get back to our true, unencumbered self. The energy work presented in this book is another support system. A support system that encourages a loving attention to body states and the feelings connected to them.

Some cultures are associated with wisdom, whereas Western culture has not traditionally been linked with wisdom. Perhaps in the turning of the wheel of time, this is where we get to go. I am interested in what wisdom feels like in a regular person, in you or me. My take on it is that it is about a big heart, lots of compassion, the ability to read one's own body signals for intuition and insight, as well as a felt connection to something larger than ourselves, be it the awe of the night sky or whatever we call Spirit.

To embody some approximation of this is to live in wholeness. The embodied state is a place of presence where in our ordinary way we get to stand in our worthiness. It seems like deep down this is what we all want, and paradoxically, without trying, it becomes a place of influence.

There is that age-old dictum "energy follows intention." In some ways, this is the essence of everything. We feel a certain way about ourselves, and that is how we manifest our life. If we are alive with esteem, then it is probable that our life will reflect the loving choices we make for ourselves with friends, partner, job, all those life choices. Of course, it is more complicated than that. Not to underestimate the layers of patterns we have laid down that have their own, perhaps subtle, perhaps not, belief systems attached to them. It is like looking at the rings of age from a section of an old-growth tree. We may be at a place in our life where the outer circles are producing good fruit, and yet the inner circles still have a story. Whatever our life looks like, my experience is that we all have a lot of catch-up work to do to realize what we are here for.

The other variable in this looking at the idea of energy-follows-intention is life itself. What a wild card. Life happens and we get to deal. Natural disasters and tragedies are in the scheme of things and have happened throughout time. These are the times that it can be invaluable to keep our wits about us. 9/11 was about the making of heroes in the moment because the situation needed individuals to rise to new levels of courage and compassion.

What is so interesting about this "new" energy medicine is that it is based on healing tradition thousands of years old. We get to come full circle. Claim our potential by bringing forward what has been used in China with the meridian flows, India with the chakra wheels, and combine it with contemporary brain research. So, we set an intention to heal, do some energy medicine for 10 minutes, notice our body experience, probably feel more ease in our body, and proceed with the day.

Our intention is our vision for what we need to feel more comfortable in our skin in our day-to-day life, as well as more resonant with our larger dreams for ourselves. For example, I may do the *Releasing Fear* protocol at a particular time because that day I am anxious about an imminent change in my life, but I also know that I carry a lot of fear and I want to release that. I might do that protocol every day during a transition and continue doing it afterwards with the intention of releasing long-held fear that contributed to my current fearfulness or anxiety.

Intention to Heal

There is now research out that DNA registers shifts in emotions. Cellular biologists are finding that the regulation and evolution of genes is a continuously dynamic process. The perception of the environment in the here and now is picked up by the cells, and the genes act accordingly. The genes are looking for signals as to whether this moment is about the stress of protection or about growth.

We also know that the happier we are, the stronger our immune system is. With biofeedback machines we can see how particular emotions correlate to particular brainwaves. At this point, it is indisputable that how we feel, our emotions, is intimately wired to our physiology. We are a hologram with individual cells containing the essence of the entire body. The body wants to heal, has an incredible ability to heal. Often it will proceed on its own, sending fresh blood and oxygen to an injured area, and several days later we feel fine. Other times, we have to get a bone set or take a medication or an herbal supplement.

Whatever is happening with the body, an intent to heal can be a powerful signal to the brain. To pair an intent with a physical gesture that goes right to the body's energetic circuitry makes it even more powerful. Most potent of all is to combine intent, physical gesture, and the feeling of wanting to heal. We step out of our way, out of any judgment we might have, and let the healing unfold. We listen in on an ongoing basis to how we are feeling in our body and heart, attune accordingly, and keep curious.

Sometimes our healing, our going for wholeness, doesn't look like we want it to. That's true. The disappointment, frustration, or anger about that becomes the next layer of healing. We work with whatever comes up. One way to work with it is to work with the protocols. Notice what is going on, find a protocol that works with those feelings, and notice if there is a difference after doing the protocol. One of the surprising things people have found about doing the protocols is that they are comforting. The body likes the experience, no matter what layer of healing we are working on.

Usually there is an initial trial period where a person is full of skepticism about the protocols and whether they really do change the body's state. This healthy skepticism is one of the best things to bring to the work. Check it out carefully and analytically to see if you feel a difference after doing a protocol. Scrutinize every time before and after doing a protocol. Among other things, this will give a moment of tuning into the body that we might not have had.

What may happen after the initial trial period is that the body looks forward to doing a protocol. This is a way to be with whatever is going on, metabolize it, and feel more ease upon completion. This is not bad for 10 minutes' time. The exquisite beauty about energy work is that it helps the body get up to speed in the moment, biochemistry changes, and it changes everything else. What we have then is the kinesthetic learning that it is safe to be in the body with feelings. We get to be with feelings without being overwhelmed or disconnected. This disrupts the patterning of trauma residue syndrome, where we feel we cannot cope effectively with life's challenges by letting us be with feelings, contain them, heal, and be soothed.

When we have the experience of being able to metabolize feelings safely, we may begin to trust the heart. Culturally, we do not lead with the heart, but with heart disease. We make our heart heavy with competitive pressure, poor food, too many material possessions, all those things that are the downside of prosperity.

It has been said that history manifests in cycles, and what is not given attention in one time period will assert itself in the next. Perhaps our collectively burdened heart is saying, "Enough, take care with the body, talk to your neighbor, be heartful in your interactions, and we will all heal."

Healing reveals the purity of the heart. The more we are loving towards ourselves in a fundamental way, the more loving kindness we spontaneously extend to our friends, family, the clerk in the grocery store. Everything is connected in a circle, and we are back to a circle: We heal with loving kindness and mindfulness, and this becomes part of the expression of who we are in the world. The more loving kindness we have for ourselves, the greater our resiliency. We go back to the heart, go back to the body, in order that everything furthers a loving stance towards self.

On an airplane, parents are advised that, if there is an emergency, they should put oxygen masks on themselves first and then their children. The parent taking care helps the child. So it is with self regard. We heal our places of unworthiness and those around us benefit. Loving kindness to self sounds like a spiritual issue, and yet I am proposing it as a physiological issue, as well as a psychological necessity in order to achieve a robust body-based sense of well-being. It doesn't matter what condition or shape our body is in, whether we are bedridden or running a marathon. This is about liking who we are, who we are in this body we inhabit. We get to work with whatever is there in the moment, be it fear, physical pain, hope-lessness, whatever is there with a kind-hearted attitude to self. This is the healing.

Building Coherence

When this stable base of compassion and love is built in, then we experience coherence. There is an awareness of body sensation, a noticing of emotion, and an ability to hold our experience without tuning out or getting frantic. We notice what is there without judg-ment, returning to the basic ground of loving kindness. We may do this by simply putting both hands on the heart and closing our eyes, breathing deeply. I believe that each of us has an enormous largely untapped reservoir of innate good, and that most of us are living decent lives that are full of distress. If we can work through the dis-tress, be with the body experience and accompanying feeling, if we can metabolize the residue of trauma we carry, we facilitate well-being and being present in all that we do. Once again, this is a place of coherence, a place of resource and regard.

What I am suggesting as an antidote to feelings of dis-ease is a hands-on approach to the body. Many of us have been impacted by trauma emotionally, physically, and/or sexually. In that process, we have come to distrust the body, not listen to it, and often to translate our discomfort into body symptoms. This does not mean we "cause" our migraines. It does mean that by not rinsing the filter of our expe-rience, keeping current, we run the risk of the body system func-tioning with one clogged filter. (Imagine not changing an oil filter on your car for years and still expecting it to run as usual.) The filter is the body itself. All of the protocols in this book address body states. Many of us have been doing therapy, body work, or both for a long time, and are still in the midst. I understand. Some of us have a longer road to walk, and the energy work shortens the distance.

Most people recovering from severe trauma have to repeatedly negotiate between a place of feeling responsible for what was done to them (or often, in the case of war, a survivor's guilt) and knowing in the here and now that one's actions have effect. This is about releasing old guilt and shame, so that we can develop a consciousness of mutuality in the present moment. Our deeds have impact. Our actions resonate like waves. Our motivation to heal benefits others. Remembering that our light gives light to others on the path. The commitment to heal, to use whatever is on our path, to awaken, is testimony of the heart's capacity to open to the mystery that we truly are.

One of the areas that therapeutic modalities often don't address adequately is the capacity to hold positive feelings. When there have been harmful experiences early on or damaging experiences later in life, the negative experiences can contaminate our perception about ourselves and discount our achievements. This minimizing of our being and of our accomplishments is a distorted, trauma-based perspective. In no way to be underestimated is the task of having the experiences we are proud of "stick" internally in order that we can resonate accurately our core worthiness. Several of the protocols address this issue. If one feels good about oneself in the moment, it is helpful to make an intent to honor that feeling, accompanying it with a physical gesture (such as *Head-Heart Hold*). This honoring helps to release from the heart old hurts, old residue, that need not be there.

When we are feeling strong emotions, positive or negative, this is the pivotal time to do energy work. When we are upset and work with the body to self-soothe in a healthy way, that disrupts the conditioning that connects agitation with alarm. Instead, there is arousal in the body, energy work, and 10 minutes later a feeling of things being lighter and less troubling. Doing this repeatedly when you are upset creates a pattern of self-care that helps new synapse strings evolve, resetting the nervous system.

Righteousness, worthiness, and deserving often come up as issues when we begin to heal. Or rather, who do we think we are to let esteem and self-care sink in? Won't that make us selfish, set us apart? A person who is comfortable in his or her skin with an open heart and a kind word for self and other is like the blue sky, a pleasure to behold.

We make choices in our life, try to control things because we need to preserve our intactness. Intactness is about how we hold ourselves together in the midst of life events. The body's confidence increases greatly when it knows there are resources to recover quickly and efficiently from daily upsets. These protocols for many people give the ability to bounce back gracefully. Confidence is about resiliency and the belief that we can effectively deal with whatever comes up.

Most of us have much resistance to being in the body, feeling our feelings, because we don't know how to do it safely, without it interfering with the rest of our life. For instance, who among us wants to consciously feel our shame? Not an inviting proposal, and yet to work with the shame releases the shame. As one person said after doing the *Releasing Shame* protocol, "there is a vast openness without shame." It may be like being by a river on a hot summer day, not wanting the shock of the cold water, but deciding to take the plunge. Doing a protocol might feel initially like diving into the cold water, but then 10 minutes later coming out cool, enjoying the warmth of the sun on the skin and the light breeze. An act of faith to begin with and 10 minutes later the senses refreshed.

I see the work as twofold: releasing the old and making way for an "unbroken wholeness." To allow our future a clear template, it is necessary to make room for it. The nervous system encodes our history, which means any developmental deficits we might have had are right here with us. It could be a holding back of our power, or a lack of trust in our ability to choose relationships wisely, or a belief that we are damaged. Again, the variations are endless. One could do a protocol to release and after the protocol the feeling could still be there, although softer. A central use for the protocols is to take static off of a feeling. The feeling itself may be what is truly going on, but the static clouds our discernment. When the static drops, we can see the situation dimensionally, with mind, heart, body functioning as one. The very work itself becomes the bridge to the new. The body learns how to metabolize what is going on and springs back with more resource. This resource gives information about the true nature of what is going on, as well as a chance to be with heartfelt feelings and body sensations. It can be the difference between feeling stuck and flowing with the situation. The internal fluidity becomes the new paradigm. This gives the possibility of more choices externally, choices that empower.

What do we need to be happy in the world? The paradigm shift is not about accepting what the media defines as happiness, but using our own barometer to point the way. We get to be visionaries. We get to speak our truth and our dreams. We get to go for it. We get to manifest heart's intention. The technique for programming new information is the same that is used to release the old: notice body sensations and feelings, state an intent to self, and proceed with gestures that key into the various energetic systems in the body. We can of course state an intent and proceed without keying into the energetic systems of the body, but it might be the difference between building a house all on one's own, versus the community pitching in and helping to build the foundation, frame the house, raise the roof. The bottom line is that it is easier the more resource we use. Mind-body integration is an amazing experience.

As world citizens of the 21st century, we get to heal our individual wounds, heal some of the hardness of daily life, and find comfort returning to the awareness of the body and the spaciousness of the heart. A parallel process to all the individual trauma is that the world is in a trauma state. This is seen in environmental degradation, violent political unrest, huge numbers of people starving, people living with AIDS. The fear of terrorism is rampant. Landfills are overflowing with our attempt to sedate our not-so-quiet desperation.

The Gaia hypothesis suggests that the earth is a living organism. Whether or not we join with that theory, what scientists of all persuasions are saying is that there is a reciprocal relating that goes on all the time. We are intimately interdependent with all that happens on this planet. One way to make our way consciously through this time is by healing individually, body and spirit, and meeting the world from that place. If we stay with our feelings about the world situation, if we acknowledge what is already there, if we work our own trauma residue, we can collectively, alchemically change the lead into gold, moving our hearts forward, using all that is as a vehicle for awakening.

This is about being straightforward with our pain, not letting it be like Muzak in the grocery store, something that is so constantly there that we barely notice it. Instead, keeping an awareness with whatever is there and noting it without judgment. The blessing is to generate loving kindness from our hurt, disowned places, some part of us knowing that the love is bigger then the pain. Each moment we can do that, we clear some of our trauma residue. To be kind to self is a way to further truthfulness, to disrupt trauma beliefs.

We participate in healing the world's trauma state by healing our own trauma residue. In that moment, in that gesture, it is our contribution to the larger whole. Every trauma pattern we work through, every moment of mindfulness goes into the stream of our collective humanity. The practice of claiming body experience is akin to saying, "I live on this planet and contribute this moment by noticing what is going on for me, being present in my body, and responding with loving kindness to self." This perspective keeps the stream free-flowing.

As human beings on this splendid planet, we all share the unavoidable experience of powerlessness. It can be in the form of natural disasters, or accidents that happen out of the blue, or the crimes of hatred and fear that we perpetuate upon each other. Life happens and on some level we have no control, no influence. It is for many of us so beyond what we can comprehend that we put it out of mind. Twelve-step programs got it right by naming this powerlessness in the first step. Begin here, at this place of giving over our illusory sense of power, and we have a chance. In the 12-step program working with addictions, it isn't about naming it once, but repeatedly going back to it, working it on an everyday level that brings change.

It is defined differently in Buddhism, but there is a similar relinquishment of self. In some kinds of Buddhist mediation practice, it is about observing with a gentle awareness, whatever arises moment to moment, noting the arising and passing of thoughts, feelings, sensation, seeing phenomena as ephemeral as bubbles.

What both of these approaches have in common is a means to respond to the influx of life that happens to us. Different tools that both further an open-hearted acceptance of the present moment.

How does the heart reconcile this powerlessness? In trauma work, the acknowledgment of powerlessness is often what is avoided at all costs. A person will assume responsibility for the harm done to them as a child rather than consider the possibility that they were the recipients of abuse, and that there was nothing they could do about it. Nothing.

A truth of our shared humanity is that we are powerless. Another truth of our shared humanity is that we are powerful. We can effect change by paying attention and acting in accord with our heart's wisdom. Once again circling back to the basic experience of sensations in the body, so that we can recognize what the body wants us to know. This might be as simple as doing energy work around discomfort in the body. The noticing and accepting of the body experience, moving to a gesture responding to that experience. For example, resting the hands on the heart as a way to listen into one's greater knowing. The gesture holding both the surrender of self and the act of listening.

In our age of specialization, it might seem odd to write about a syndrome that applies to us all. The wheel of life is turning, and we are returning to the awareness of the heart. The heart contains us all. The heart awareness is about the kinship of all beings, and the interconnectedness of all deeds. We all get to heal. We all get to awaken to our true self. In this moment, we turn the wheel. Blessings to us all.

2.

Developing a Language of Energy Gestures

As young ones, we learn language to the delight of our parents. Language gives us another means to discover the world around us. It gives us the power to name and to express. Later, adopting the language of our peer group gives us a way to belong. It shores up our sense of identity. There is a parallel process with learning the language of energy gestures, which key into the energetic circuitry of the body either by touch or visualization.

The body's energy circuitry has been mapped for us in chakras and in acupuncture meridians and points. As a culture, we've reached a certain comfort with these concepts, particularly with acupuncture. Many of us know that meridians are pathways of energy that connect a network of points. In fact, acupuncture has become so mainstream in Western society that a growing number of health insurance policies cover it. Chakras are less well known in this country, but I suspect that may change.

The power centers of life-force described in the energy meridians, points, and chakras provide an excellent way to generate healing energy. You can feel it yourself. The palms of your hands contain chakras. If you rub your hands together and then pull them apart, you can feel the energy between them. In many religious traditions, the palms of the hands are touching as a gesture of reverence. Combine this ancient knowledge with brain research and returning to the heart, and we have a way to respond to the weariness of our cares that revitalizes.

Tuning into the energy circuitry of the body gives us a vehicle for our hopes and prayers for our creative, true self. In Jin Shin acupressure, the idea is to hold two points at the same time to harmonize the functions of the meridians. In the protocols, I am including chakras and the combination of chakra and acupressure point in this method of holding two points as a way to bring life force and balance to the areas being held. (If you have an injury at any of the points or you find them uncomfortable to reach, visualize white light touching the chakra or point instead of touching it with your hands.)

Learning a new language, particularly one that includes not just words but also skills, takes practice and patience. To start on this road of energy medicine, it helps to become broadly familiar with the vocabulary of chakras, selected acupressure points, and certain key gestures.

Chakras

Chakras are energy wheels of vitality. There are many in the body, but seven are primary. What follows is the briefest naming of them in order to have a context for and some understanding of the intention behind the holding gestures presented in this book.

The root chakra is located at the base of the spine. This chakra is concerned with survival issues. A person who has confidence around survival issues can thrive. There is a feeling of stability and well being. The person meets the world with assurance and ease. When a protocol involves putting a hand on the sacrum (the base of the spine), it is helping to activate these qualities. This chakra is about grounding, furthering strength and resilience in the body, opening to the joy of being alive.

The second chakra is located below the navel in the region of the lower abdomen. For martial art practitioners, this is the center of gravity, the location for breathing with power. The second chakra is about flowing energy, sexual energy, creative energy, energy that for each person contains male and female aspects. A fun place if it is

Primary chakras

undamaged. Many people speak of our culture as being overzealous with striving, and thus often third chakra dominant. I don't disagree, but my take on it is that for many of us in this culture, our second chakra is where we carry our wounds. With that in mind, many of the protocols have a hand on the second chakra. This activates the creative life force, desire, feelings, and the deep healing of the body.

The third chakra is located at our solar plexus, above the navel, below the breastbone. This chakra is about drive, ambition, accomplishment. It is from this chakra that a person develops discipline and a clean will if the chakra is balanced. It is the solar disc of the body. All the chakras need the energy of other chakras to be aligned, but the third chakra *really* needs the connection with other chakras. This chakra needs the fluidity of the second chakra and the open-heartedness of the fourth chakra to shine. It is a luminous place in the body, if the energy is not too tight, or conversely stagnant.

The fourth chakra is the heart center. As you would expect, this chakra is all about love, all kinds of love: unconditional love, intimate love, love between friends. It is the seat of compassion, generosity, kindness. This is the place of our inner connectedness with all beings. A good life begins with healthy esteem, which is the territory of the fourth chakra. Every protocol begins with heart energy by way of the *Simple Balance,* which is detailed in the next chapter.

The fifth chakra is the throat. This chakra governs communication and expression. It is about speaking one's truth. In harmony, this chakra provides a fine interplay between listening and speaking. Harmonic patterns, rhythm, vibration are also connected to the throat chakra. In some ways, this chakra is the gatekeeper between our interior self and how we work and play in the world.

The sixth chakra is the third eye slightly above the bridge of the nose between the eyebrows. This is the chakra connected to intuition, the place of seeing with the mind's eye. This high level of perception can be an extraordinary protection giving a person a "sixth sense" to discern a situation. Traditionally this chakra is associated with the power of inner light to see clearly. In many of the protocols, this chakra is included as a vehicle to bring forward our unique vision.

The seventh chakra is located at the top of the head. This crown chakra is connected to our higher knowing and our spirituality. This chakra is about the delight and light of the spirit manifest in the world. It is about wisdom, while the wisdom body is the body with all the chakras open and aligned, working together as a team. This then becomes the place of manifestation.

The energetic centers of the body function like the body as a whole does, that is, as a system. To have optimum potential of the whole is to recognize the inner connectedness of the parts. The protocols encourage a dynamic communication between the chakras, facilitating free-flowing energy.

Acupuncture Points

Acupuncture points are places on the body where vital energy flows and can be accessed and influenced. The protocols in this book focus on a number of acupressure points, also called potent points.

1. *Four Whites St2* is located about one inch below the center of the eye. Tapping this point if you are overwhelmed or flooded with emotion can calm the spirit very quickly.

2. *Middle of a Person GV26* is located midway between the end of the nose and the upper lip. This is the endpoint of the governing vessel meridian. Touching this point increases brain function by furthering alertness and concentration.

3. *Receiving Starch CV24* is located in the dip of the chin below the lower lip. Tapping this point firms up a sense of self and metab-

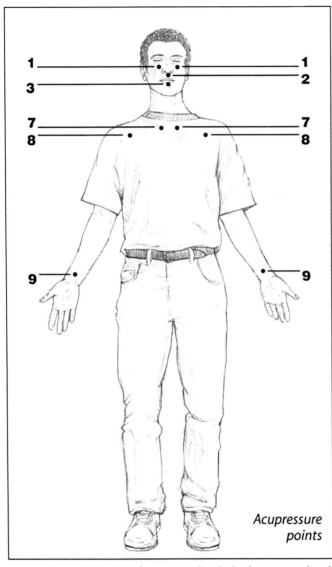

1
3
7
8
9

1
2
7
8
9

Acupressure points

olizes shame. This is the end point of the conception vessel meridian.

4. *Gates of Consciousness GB20* is located below the occipital bone in the hollow at the edge of the trapezius muscle. A hand on the back of the head covers both GB20 and B10. Touching this point helps with hypertension, shock to the body, exhaustion.

5. *Heavenly Pillar B10* is located below the base of the skull in the middle of the trapezius muscle. A hand on the back of the head covers both GB20 and B10. Touching this point eases anxiety, stress, stiff neck, and generally relaxes the body.

6. *Wind Block TW17* is located in the hollow behind the earlobe. Touching this point helps to regulate the thyroid gland, as well as to metabolize emotional distress. This point is contacted with the *Eyelid Sweep,* which helps to calm hyperarousal or alarm.

7. *Elegant Mansion K27* is located at the hollow where the breast bone joins with the collar bone. Rubbing this point will bring energy, vitality, and clearness to the body.

8. *Letting Go Lu1* is located on the outer part of the chest three finger widths below the collar bone between the second and third rib. Rubbing this point helps relieve emotional distress and helps facili-

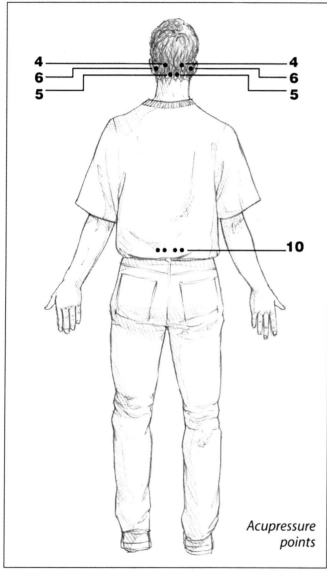

4 —————— 4
6 —————— 6
5 —————— 5

10

Acupressure points

tate emotional relaxation.

9. *Inner Gate P6* is located on the palm side of the forearm, two-and-one-half finger widths from the wrist crease between the tendons. Touching or tapping this point benefits digestion (a controlling point for the chest to navel area), and gives peace to the spirit.

10. *Sea of Vitality B23, B47* is located on the back at waist level, two to four finger widths away from the spine between the second and third lumbar vertebrae. This area opposite the navel is also called Ming Men and has influence over the adrenal glands and kidneys. Rubbing this point, provided you have no injury, helps to tonify the immune system and ease depression, depletion, and fear.

Gestures

Just as words can open up whole new worlds, energy gestures can be a bridge between a "meaningless" symptom and the body's wisdom. By working the body's energy points and pathways with gestures, you can help to process trauma residue and differentiate between trauma residue and true self. Energy gestures can make everyday life easier by removing some of the residual distress that we all carry.

Another word you may hear to describe these gestures is *mudra.* Mudras have been around for thousands of years and appear in many cultures. In a basic sense, a mudra is a hand gesture that conveys meaning. Sometimes it involves tapping a certain place on the body. Sometimes it involves holding a certain place on the body. Sometimes it involves making a feathering action over a certain place

Crown-Heart

on the body. A mudra involves symbolic meaning moving into greater wholeness. Eastern religious traditions use mudras often. And they are found in yoga and in artistic venues, such as dance.

The mudras—hand gestures—used in the this book are intended to give form to a focus that furthers self actualization. They are intended to access a deeper knowing. In this book, I am bringing forward the gesture of mudras while synthesizing them with work connected to the heart and the brain.

A heart mudra involves any touching of the heart with one or both hands. Or it may involve tapping the pericardium meridian. The heart mudras are *Crown-Heart Hold, Double-Hands Heart Hold, Forehead-Heart Hold, Head-Heart Hold, Heart Glide, Gate to Peace, Heart Blessing,* and *Going for Gold.* The brain mudras are *Brain Flow, Middle-Ground,* and *Wise Brain.*

Double-Hands Heart

In *Crown-Heart Hold,* you hold one hand on the crown of your head and one hand on your heart. This position says to the body, "I can be with the wisdom of my heart." In some spiritual traditions, this is about the "awakened heart."

In *Double-Hands Heart Hold,* you hold both hands on the heart. This position says to the body, "I am in my heart. This openness is my strength."

In *Forehead-Heart Hold,* you hold one hand on your forehead and one hand on your heart. This position says to the body, "I can see what I need to see and bring it into my heart." This mudra is a way to further consciousness,

Forehead-Heart

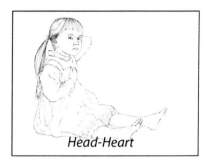

Head-Heart

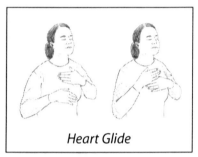

Heart Glide

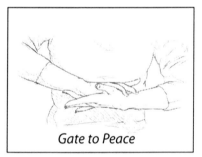

Gate to Peace

Heart Blessing

with a hand on the prefrontal cortex, and compassion, with a hand on the heart.

In *Head-Heart Hold,* you hold one hand on the back of your head and one hand on your heart. This position says to the body, "It is okay to soften and release. It is okay to rest in the heart."

In *Heart Glide,* you glide one hand after the other in a downward direction over your heart. This action gently soothes the heart. In the Sufi tradition, it is done to cleanse the heart.

In *Gate to Peace,* you begin by folding your forearms in front of your chest and then sliding your arms outward until your palms are aligned, facing each other. Then you alternate tapping with the middle finger just below the wrist crease for about one minute. This action provides bilateral stimulation of the brain while connecting with the pericardium meridian, which governs the heart, thus opening the heart and balancing the brain.

In *Heart Blessing,* your hands are crossed over your chest and you alternate tapping with each hand for one to two minutes to balance left and right hemispheres. The hands are tapping on Lung 1, which is named Letting Go because when stimulated it facilitates release of emotional distress.

Going for Gold is a combination gesture with the first part being one hand on the thymus under the collarbone and one hand on the heart. The second part being both hands on the heart. It has as an intent to find gratitude in the wisdom and spaciousness of the heart. It is useful as an everyday gesture to center and to open. It is useful with any intent. It is useful as a way to begin the day and as a way to end the day.

In *Brain Flow Mudra,* you hold one hand on the back of the head and one hand on the forehead to connect the prefrontal cor-

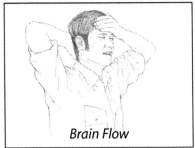

Brain Flow

Middle-Ground

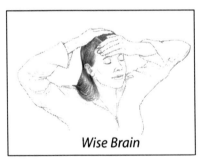

Wise Brain

tex to the fight, flight, or freeze response in the back of the brain. This pivotal energy tool provides an energy flow between these two areas. It helps to synthesize information, feeling states, and new understandings. Maintain the hold for about two minutes or until you feel a pulsing and/or heat in your hands.

In *Middle-Ground Mudra,* you hold a hand on the crown and a hand on the back of the head, facilitating communication with the brain stem, sometimes referred to as the lizard brain and the deep knowing of the crown chakra. This is helpful to negotiate a practical path between fight, flight, or freeze response and our highest good.

In *Wise Brain Mudra,* you hold one hand on the forehead and one hand on the crown, connecting the sixth and seventh chakras, pituitary and pineal glands. This is a way to access deeper seeing and knowing.

Developing a repertoire of responses to the body is like having many words to describe a beautiful day, each adjective cogent and descriptive in its own right. In this book, the energy gestures are combined into protocols. It's valuable to use an energy gesture for a couple of minutes wherever you are upset, and it is also valuable to use longer sequences, 10 minutes or so, as a way for the body to free itself from some of the habitual conditioning that affects us all.

You may not necessarily be focused on past trauma but would like a way to help make it through the day without feeling overwhelmed. Or a big life event happens and you have big feelings. By engaging the power and wisdom already held in your body, the gestures, the protocols, can help you feel safe and fluid while negotiating life's challenges.

It is interesting that chakra centers and acupressure points are connected, as shown in the table on the next page. Indeed, energy

How chakras and acupressure points connect

First chakra	⟶ B27-34 Sacral Points
Second chakra	⟶ CV6 Sea of Energy
Third chakra	⟶ CV12 Center of Power
Fourth chakra	⟶ CV17 Sea of Tranquility
Fifth chakra	⟶ CV22 Heavenly Rushing
Sixth chakra	⟶ GV24.5 Third Eye Point
Seventh chakra	⟶ GV21 Anterior Summit and GV20 One Hundred Meeting Point

centers throughout the body are meant to be hooked up. One of the most important examples is in the brain. If the left and right hemispheres of the brain are hooked up, it allows for the free flow of energy in other parts of the body.

Brain lateralization is the term used when the left and right hemispheres are unbalanced. In brain synchrony, when the hemispheres are balanced, high-end learning and resiliency can take place. Emotionally, it is the difference between feeling cut off and feeling integrated, "all together." The unified brain begets a person with open-ended resource. The protocols provide a way to support the nervous system while acclimating to whole brain functioning.

This is what informs systems theory: Respond to one part of the system, and it has a ripple effect on the other parts of the system. The benefit of using the protocols is in the felt shift after doing a protocol; in other words, you feel different. This experiential change in the feeling of the body is the bottom line. The gestures give the possibility of hooking up previously disconnected states of being. For example doing *Brain Flow Mudra* (one hand on the forehead, one hand on the back of the head) when you are agitated may, in a few minutes, give a sense of quiet to the entire body.

I think of it this way. Some plant nurseries have large carts on which you can haul plants, even trees, without much struggle. Having unbalanced brain hemispheres is like having a magnificent tree on your cart, struggling to get the cart to the front of the nursery, and discovering once you arrive that the hand brake has been on. When brain hemispheres are balanced, it's like having the hand brake off and rolling along, a free-flowing movement that takes little effort.

The bilateral stimulation of the brain happens in four ways in this book: *Heart Blessing, Gate to Peace, Eye Opener,* and *Gold-White Weave.* The first three involve motion going from one side of the body to the other, and back again. *Gold-White Weave* involves visualizing light in the brain.

As we learn and develop, as trauma residue is worked, new neural connections form. We may be temporarily overwhelmed with chaos, but because of an inherent dynamic ability to work the chaos, the system emerges with increased strength and viability. The chaos in an open system creates flow. The chaos in a closed system produces stagnation. In this context, this means that the very act of making a mind-body connection in the midst of distress propels a person along the continuum towards an open system model. The more we metabolize trauma residue, the more we condition the brain to adapt to complex, fulfilling ways of functioning. We grow by working our pain, and the brain grows with us.

Speaking the Language

Each of the gestures that make up the protocols in this book has a particular function. Together, the gestures accomplish the purpose of the protocol; the protocol gives a rhythm to the gestures. Most people are interested in how one protocol achieves one objective and another protocol achieves another objective. In one way, it is like having a dictionary of words, selecting certain words corresponding to what one wants to convey, and putting them together in a sentence form. Let's look at one protocol and see how it is put together. *Songs of the Heart* is about attachment to others and the implicit vulnerability that happens as a result of caring for another. In our life course and attachment to others, we will also experience grief. This protocol is designed to keep the heart open and release the grief. The first three steps all involve heart mudras because that is the source of our connection to others. The fourth step, *Synapse to Synapse* (massaging K27 at the top of the sternum while having a hand on the heart) is about feeling centered in the body. The fifth step, *Gold-White Weave* is about having the brain, the feeling and thinking, function as one system. As a generalization, the first several steps of a protocol are about working the material while the last steps are about stabilizing the benefit in the body experience.

A protocol with a different aim is *Emotional First Aid*. This protocol is useful in a crisis. It is all about regulating feelings that seem out of hand. It starts with *Back Again*. Tapping the thymus and chin is such an aid for restoring body cohesion in the midst of big feelings. The protocol goes onto *Basic Relief* (one hand on the forehead, one hand underneath the nose). Okay, so now to get back to mental clarity. From there, to *Eyelid Sweep* which calms the triple warmer meridian and soothes at the same time. Next up, is *Brain Flow Mudra* to integrate the probable physiological shift. Ending with *Solid Ground* (massaging under the eye, with one hand on the sacrum) for grounding and stability. So here is the sequence: return to being in the body, facilitate mental alertness, calm the fight or flight response, integrate and ground.

As you see, the gestures in each protocol are arranged to accomplish the purpose of the protocol. However, this is not a fixed melody. When you are doing a protocol, improvising is just fine. Simply listen in to your intuitive signals and follow them. You may wish to change one of the steps of a protocol to another energy gesture because it feels right. In other words, substitution and adaptation are just fine.

For instance, some people don't like tapping, so tapping the chin and thymus in *Back Again* would not be helpful. Holding these points, however, might be just the ticket. Another example is the hands moving down over the chest in the *Heart Glide*. For some people, that motion is not comfortable, whereas both hands on the heart for them is effective and soothing. As a rule of thumb, try doing the protocols as written a couple of times and see how it goes. There are protocols that ease agitation which will most probably provide immediate relief, and there are protocols that help to take the static out of the system so that one can go deeper. An example of the latter is *Releasing Shame.* If the protocol is working, the shame will be less and there will be other feelings available. The criterion here is about richness and range of feeling.

One way to see how a gesture, let's say *Eye Opener,* is working is to do it every day for a week. Notice what happens, how your body feels before and after doing it. Many people do this with full protocols as well; choose one and explore it over a period of time, say daily for a couple of weeks. This option has the advantage of comfort and familiarity. *Five-Step Flow* is a good place to start because it probably is the most versatile protocol. Or perhaps it would be more helpful to do some bilateral stimulation of the brain, like *Eye Opener,* or a soothing gesture like *Eyelid Sweep,* or to hold your hands on a chakra that doesn't feel balanced.

In Part 3, you'll find a key to help you choose protocols that address specific intents. Or you can look at the Purpose section in each protocol and see which one best matches what you need at the moment. As you become more familiar with them, the most helpful choices will become apparent.

One of the most critical aspects of working with the individual gestures and with the full protocols is the initial balancing. For energy gestures to achieve their full potency, it's vital that the body have some measure of biochemical stability and that the energy between the right and left hemispheres is efficiently crossing over. This is why each protocol starts with the *Simple Balance;* it addresses these issues. If you only have time for one thing, do the *Simple Balance.* We may underestimate how chronically stressed we are and not realize we are out of balance. Repeated or prolonged stress wears at cohesion. These are some straightforward ways to center and ground. From there we get to discover a new pattern that develops when a person maintains body coherence over time.

What if in a given day many distressing things have happened, and you are wanting to do a protocol, but not knowing which one to choose. One way to go is to identify the strongest feelings and choose a protocol that works with that. There are six protocols listed in the index for distress. All of them have as an intent to help ease the overwhelming feelings. Or if you have a practice of doing one protocol each day, continue doing that one. By working to metabolize whatever is going on, the learned pathways and protective responses of the body get an opportunity to be reset. This is about addressing the guarding of the body that wants to keep feelings in and new information out. The re-education is about having high stimulation and not closing down. The protocols provide a means to stay in awareness with whatever is going on. The amazing thing about awareness is that it makes things mutable. We can facilitate change and have grace in the broken places by keeping in awareness and responding kindly to the body.

We all know the experience of being out of sync with the body physically and also emotionally. We may close down for instance as a way to stay protected. We close our heart, so we won't be hurt. The paradigm shifts if there is a way to be open and stay protected at the same time. Animals rely on instinct to stay alive. If our ability to listen in to our intuitive radar is keen, we can rely on that. These energy tools are gestures of the heart, ways to become more present in the body, polishing our ability to intuitively know what is best for us.

Other Terms

In addition to the language of chakras, acupuncture, and mudras, you may encounter a number of other important concepts and gestures as well, such as these.

DNA Breath

Coherence: This is about a clear, open access to body signals, confident that you have the resources to respond to them, and a baseline comfort in your skin. It is the physical manifestation of working through emotional distress.

Discharge: In this context it is wiggling the toes, shaking the hands out, or massaging the earlobes.

DNA breath: In this breath, you begin breathing in from

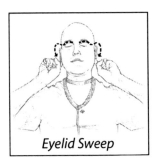

Eyelid Sweep

the sacrum (base of the spine) tracing a spiral with the breath to the crown, on the exhale breathing out an overlapping spiral, creating replications of the life-giving double-helix DNA.

Eyelid sweep: A practice that starts with an index finger at the corner of each eye, gently pulling the fingers over the eyelids, across the temple, and around the back of the earlobes, and then starting over again. This is usually done 10 to 20 times. This practice can be calming and reassuring when you feel uncomfortable arousal.

Exhale: This can be anything from the sweetness of a sigh to a breathing practice that has a longer exhale than inhale. In any case, letting go.

Learnings: The heart's wisdom that you write down, often after a protocol. It is an intuitive message that is given words so that the body information can be kept conscious.

Potentiate: To combine one energy gesture with another for greater result. You'll learn more about potentiating energy gestures in Chapter 3.

Prayer: Larry Dossey, in his book *Reinventing Medicine,* defines the coming era of medicine as "a form of healing based on the fundamental, infinite nature of consciousness." Prayer is a nonlocal way of connecting with the divine. Prayer can be a way to begin any of the protocols, asking for protection, guidance, awareness, awakening.

Presence: This is to be in the body, with felt sensations, with awareness, with loving kindness connected to feelings of the heart that are arising and passing moment after moment.

Sideways Figure-8

Sideways figure-8 eye movement: This is a powerful tool to connect the hemispheres of the brain by moving the eyes upper right, lower right, upper left, lower left, and back again to upper right. This is very useful for unfolding feeling, as well as integrating disruptive states.

Simple balance: This two-minute centering tool begins with drink-

Spacious Heart Breath

ing water, from there hooking up the hemispheres with *Heart Blessing* and ending with *Double-Hands Heart Hold,* resting the attention on the heart for a moment. It starts every protocol.

Somatically accessed wisdom (SAW): SAW is about befriending the body and opening the vision based on the protocols in this book, which work with brain, heart, and body to focus healing energy and allow the body's innate wisdom to come forward.

Spacious heart breath: This is about breathing into the heart center and, with the breath, tracing an infinity symbol (a sideways figure-8) and breathing out the heart center.

Tonglen: A Buddhist practice of breathing in our discomfort and breathing out loving kindness. The adaptations on this concept are endless. Tonglen profoundly disrupts conditioning by taking into our body what is hard to experience and giving out to the world the lightness and spaciousness we want to hold onto.

Thymus tap: The thymus can be activated by lightly tapping the point where the second rib joins the breastbone. John Diamond, in his book *Your Body Doesn't Lie,* speaks of the thymus gland as the link between mind and body, *thymos* from the Greek being translated as life force or seat of life energy. Tapping the thymus can ease the body when you feel distress.

Trauma residue syndrome (TRS): This is a condition where a person feels depleted by life's challenges and develops stress responses. TRS is a physiological state where old truths, places of deep conditioning, can have more power than new truths. The cellular memory of a previous trauma state rising to the surface, thereby increasing the intensity of daily life.

Visualization of light: The body seems to like having light inside as well as outside. Visualization can involve light being drawn from the crown to the heart center and then radiating to all the cells of the

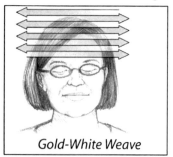
Gold-White Weave

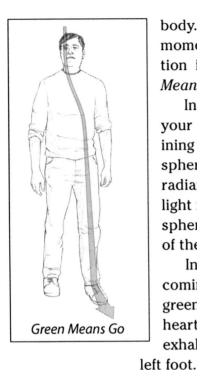

Green Means Go

body. Whatever color of light you feel most drawn to at the moment can be used. Two different examples of visualization in the protocols are *Gold-White Weave* and *Green Means Go.*

In *Gold-White Weave,* you imagine gold light going from your right to your left hemisphere, at the same time imagining white light going from your left to your right hemisphere, the golden white light overlapping and forming a radiant weave of light, filling your entire brain. The gold light represents the richness of emotion of the right hemisphere; the white light represents incisive understanding of the left hemisphere.

In *Green Means Go,* you imagine healing green light coming into your right hemisphere with the inhale, the green light picking up any trauma residue, traveling to the heart, continuing to pick up trauma residue, and on the exhale going down your left leg and out the sole of your left foot.

Whole-brain functioning: Using the analytical, verbal left hemisphere and the creative, intuitive right hemisphere in a balanced way. The sum is greater than the parts: Whole-brain functioning facilitates open-ended potential.

Whole-brain functioning with SAW: Touching acupressure points is not new. Holding chakras is not new. The distinction here is about returning to the heart with these heart-centered practices that engage connection to the body. There are 12 notes in a scale. From the 12 notes, countless melodies are created. These particular gestures are what I call "Songs of Manifestation."

3.

Using the Protocols

One thing a lot of us share is wanting to get it right. This stern internal voice can influence much of what we do and may make you feel that you want to pick the "right" protocol and do it in the "right" way. But there's another way to view this. The catalyst for healing may indeed be a particular protocol. Or it may be the very place of choosing to heal that helps to catalyze. In other words, the personal intent that you bring to the work influences how your body works the protocol. Your body gets the big picture and knows how to adjust from there.

To be sure, the protocols in this book are designed with a specific intent in mind, and they are useful in that regard. In fact, at the end of this chapter you'll find a key to which protocols may be most helpful in working with a variety of feelings and concepts. For example, if you are angry and you do the *Emotional First Aid* protocol, your anger most probably will diminish. Or if you're having a repetitive thought that's uncomfortable, you may choose to do the *Moving Through Intrusive Thoughts, Moving to Insight* protocol. There's a good chance that you will feel more centered, more in control, after doing the protocol.

If you're uncertain about which protocol to use, look through them and see if you sense a resonance with the purpose of a particular protocol and what you feel you need in the moment. Or see if you have an intuitive draw to a protocol. Over time, you probably will feel a "honing in" to which protocol would provide the greatest benefit in the moment and whether you might do the protocol once or perhaps every day for a couple of weeks.

In the process of selecting protocols, you may find yourself undergoing a paradigm shift in which your sense of wanting to get it right shifts into a sense of wondering about the sensations in your body, no right or wrong, only a path that leads home. Let this spirit of discovery—of getting to the protocol and of doing the protocol—be the guide.

As you become more familiar with the protocols and the process of choosing and doing them, you may want to try combining the various energy gestures based on your own instincts. Combining one energy gesture with another may give you an even more powerful result. In other words, combining gestures may potentiate the result. Combinations that I have developed for the protocols are as follows:

Back Again, shown on the left below, combines tapping of the thymus and chin to give resiliency and cohesion to the body. Many people have a strong preference for just having several fingers on the chin instead of tapping. This is just fine; it works just as well and can be more soothing.

Basic Relief, on the right, combines one hand on the forehead and

Back Again

Basic Relief

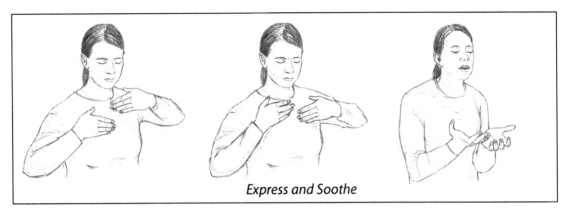

Express and Soothe

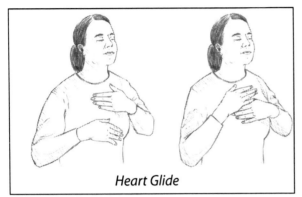

Heart Glide

Eye Opener

one hand beneath the nose (on the GV26 point) to disperse confusion and anxiety and provide centering and balancing when there is too much mental activity.

Express and Soothe combines feathering (tapping from the middle to the top of the sternum and exhaling through the mouth) with the *Heart Glide* (one hand after another gliding down over the heart) to release particularly painful feelings or feelings that have been obstructed and feel congested.

Eye Opener combines sideways figure-8 eye movement with hands on the heart to help to center and calm the body, restoring cohesion.

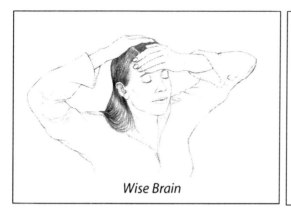

Wise Brain

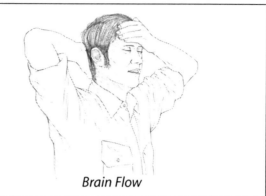

Brain Flow

Laser Like combines *Wise Brain Mudra,* on the left above, and *Brain Flow Mudra,* on the right, to spark insight and further mental clarity.

Solid Ground, shown on the left below, combines massaging under the eyes (at the St2 point) with the thumb and index finger while holding the other hand on the sacrum to help settle energy in the body and regulate anxiety.

Synapse to Synapse, on the right, combines holding one hand on K27 (the kidney 27 point), which is in the hollow below the collarbone next to the breastbone, while holding the other hand on the heart. Some people prefer to just have a hand over both points and a hand on the heart. Yes, this is just fine. This helps to clear, balance,

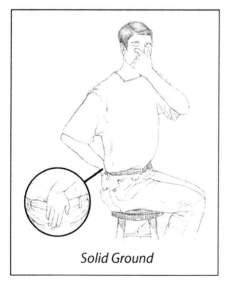

Solid Ground

Synapse to Synapse

and stabilize the body's energy.

Many people find combining heartfelt intent with a silent invocation before beginning any kind of healing work helps to further what happens. This is another way to deepen a loving stance towards self. Over and over, I name the heart as what we are to return to. I do this unabashedly, and yet, I also have concern, because in our culture the heart is trivialized. It seems we go from one extreme to the other, either having the heart be about sentimentality or at the other end an ironic disdain. What I am talking about is the accountability of cultivating joy and gratitude. Simply, living our daily life with a clear, open heart to honor our time on this splendid planet.

Cultivate Intent

One of the most frequently asked questions about the protocols has to do with intent, or what exactly to think about while doing a protocol. There are two answers to this question. The first is that each protocol has a section called "Purpose," where the intent of the protocol is stated. By selecting a particular protocol, you have already established an intent. The second answer is that you can select a protocol and name for yourself a more defined intent that is best suited to the moment. Then, say that intent with each step of the protocol. Both ways work.

An intent is a place where we get to utilize the whole brain, bringing the heart's desire forward with the right hemisphere and actualizing it in the world with the resources of the left hemisphere. A dream or vision needs a practical thoughtfulness to manifest. With the empowerment of furthering an intent, we move through a threshold that helps to stabilize whole-brain functioning.

The richness of working with an intent, of finding our place in the world, is that it has a dynamic flow: creating and releasing, creating and releasing, over and over again. This informs how we negotiate the tension between power and powerlessness. There is the experience of open-ended potential that interfaces with something mysterious and huge. Another way to say it is that this is about knowing the difference between what we can influence and where we need to let go. An example is a parent conscientiously raising a child and then relinquishing influence as the child moves into the world and discovers his or her own path.

Open the Heart

The heart is in many ways the guardian of our spirit. When we are hurt, emotionally or physically, the heart is on the front line doing all it can to keep us protected. This may mean that it shuts down at times in order to titrate, make a situation manageable. Sometimes as a guardian, the heart forgets to open back up to full capacity. In psychological language, this is about overwhelming experiences and trauma responses that become wired into the nervous system. By responding directly to the heart—the gatekeeper so to speak—with an intent and a physical gesture, the heart gets a chance to open to the present moment. Mindfulness of an intent and loving kindness in a charged moment are more powerful than trauma conditioning.

Self-compassion, the ability to respond with tenderness to self with any feeling of hurt or pain, lets one drop into the body and heart. It's as if we are living slightly outside of our body with all the stimulation of our culture, and our busy lives, let alone trauma residue.

Taking a moment to respond with care and curiosity to what we are feeling is a way of honoring our basic humanness. I believe the big picture for us all is about actualizing self-love. This capacity to love self is based on knowing self, knowing how our trauma residue manifests. We get to identify learned pathways and protective responses in the body, do a protocol, and re-educate the nervous system by pairing an old feeling place with a body-based response that takes the edge off.

Trust the Body's Creative Wisdom

Symptoms of distress are signals trying to communicate. A sort of Morse code is going on all the time. One of the difficulties when there is past trauma is that chronic shame can interfere with us receiving the signals. So, the first task is to work with clearing the background shame. The shame is a sticky place because it is often so pervasive we don't even know it's there. How an individual expresses shame is a very unique matter. For some, it may be around body issues, for some around areas of motivation, for others it may be connected to some kind of addiction. A general across-the-board indication is feeling ill at ease emotionally or physically much of the time. Being comfortable in one's skin, a place of harmony, balance, and esteem, is the antithesis of shame. As shame decreases, cohesion increases. It's that simple.

The shame, a signal of distress, is a call to healing, just as other signals are a call to healing. It is almost a commonplace story about someone getting cancer, working to understand what they were not actualizing, and then going for it. The individual person may live or die. The story in this regard is about finding the missing piece and living it, not letting it be split off from their lives.

Signals are like lanterns in the dark, illuminating what we can't quite see without them. Attuning to the signals provides a means to understand our story and move forward.

Bring Trauma and Darkness to the Light

The gathering together of the light and the dark is about acknowledging the totality of who we are. The challenge when there has been trauma is that we can interpret the experience as us being bad. If we can keep our heart open to our basic goodness, then we can differentiate when we mess up from being a "bad" person. Of course, this is easier said than done. One thing that helps is to have one gesture that brings us back into our body when we feel stirred or triggered by something going on. It could be any gesture that we have an affinity to, like both hands on the heart, or some variation of bilateral stimulation of the brain like alternating tapping of the feet. Something that we can do unobtrusively for a minute or so anyplace.

So much of our shadow darkness—rage, fear, acting out—is informed by injury. We have been hurt and developed a pattern reaction to events that evoke the origin of our pain. This pattern response can be a voice calling for compassion if we look underneath the surface. What does this experience remind us of? In our associations to this experience, has there been a time when we felt powerless and injured?

One way to work with feelings of powerlessness is to do the protocol *Five-Step Flow* on a regular basis with the intent, "I accept the powerlessness I experienced in my trauma." If truly felt, this can open to grief, to a place of letting grief wash through. It can be like a hard rain that after a few minutes clears and revitalizes. This practice might need the support of therapy to do, but opening the door to our previous powerlessness can be a linchpin piece in recovering our true self.

Generate Loving Kindness for Self

Much is written about the extraordinary value of forgiving others. Yes, and what might have even more potency is the practice of forgiving self. The heart contains the totality of self. It's all there. We get to see, to witness, all that we do, all that we think and feel, to repair or make amends as needed, and to return to the boundless loving heart that is our basic nature. Attuning to the abiding loving kindness that is always there, we deepen our relationship to self, to others, and to the world.

The fact of the matter is that we are diminished by hate, aggression, rage, and fear-based responses. The discovery working with the heart is that it can all be noticed, whatever comes up, and used as a vehicle for compassion.

The protocols, the energy work presented in this book, are one means to metabolize this trauma residue. For sure, it can be a long haul and yet we generate loving kindness in the very act of doing our individual inner work, going for our right to heal and to be whole. From this place, we get to meet the wonder of the world with our hearts open.

Do the Simple Balance

Coherence is the open-hearted grounding in the body. From this place, we can cultivate a clean power to fully claim our innate capacity for good. What is needed for there to be coherence is for the body to be balanced. Before doing a protocol, use the *Simple Balance* to prepare and get grounded:

Heart Blessing

Start by drinking water. Water is essential for conducting electrical impulses in the body. When we are dehydrated, the body goes into a physiological stress response that interferes with focus and perception. This basic gesture of drinking water can provide physiological harmony to the nervous system.

Then move on to the *Heart Blessing.* With hands crossed over the chest, alternately tap with each hand to balance left and right hemispheres of the brain. This gesture is about hooking up the hemispheres, bilateral stimulation of the brain, while tapping on the acupressure point Lung 1 at the outer part of the chest, which facilitates emotional release. The mind cannot think straight and the body cannot feel clearly when the left and right hemispheres are disconnected. This is about helping the brain function with its inherent wholeness.

Double-Hands Heart Hold

Now do the *Double-Hands Heart Hold:* Rest in the heart for a moment with both hands on the heart. Taking a moment to rest in the heart, letting one's attention be with the sensation of the hands over the heart, is about furthering a heart-centered awareness, resting in the heart's capacity to hold all feelings without judgment and generating a deep compassion for self. This is the grace of being in the body and letting the presence of the heart be felt. It doesn't matter what the feelings are. What matters is the hands on the heart saying, "I'm here."

The *Simple Balance* can be done anytime, anywhere, with or without protocols. The key is remembering to check in with self at various times throughout one's day to see if some kind of balancing is needed. If indeed we are here to fulfill our unique potential, then it is helpful to be onboard with optimum resource. Our innate capacity for good emerges with the integrity of power claimed through an open-heartedness, a relating of one human being to another, a seeing with the heart.

Part II.

What We Are Here For

4.

Cornerposts of Healing

The next four chapters (*Shadow Blessed By Light, The Loved Body, Help Is On The Way,* and *The Everyday Luminous Self*) are the four cornerposts of healing. We all have time of anxiety or crisis; we all have distress that we don't process; we all have physical symptoms; for most of us we have moments of gratitude and rejoicing. How do we make this all of one piece? How do we claim power and clarity in our regular life situations? How do we open to our true, deep self?

Self-help is often demeaned and dismissed as somehow being "less than." Less than what? It may be a time to proclaim the term as a banner that says yes to all that is within: a range of feeling and magnitude of power like none other. Self-help is generating wisdom and resource from our own experience.

All this expansive talk, all this furthering around flourishing may seem lofty. The words here may have a resonance with you, they may not. In fact, you may wish that there were more examples, more practical stories. This writing is only a conduit to the protocols – there you have the direct experience from your body. The template of what we are here for is in the body experience and seeing with the heart. In that place of attuning, we can call on joyful manifestation. The power comes from a congruence with body, mind, and spirit. We listen in, feel sensations, feel feelings, allow insight, and move from there. With willingness, the world is available.

We all have character structure. It can be defined as an accumulation of habits we have used to make it through and how some of the tendencies become solidified into our identity. This can be a fairly narrow bandwidth. We all have unworked material. Unworked material gets woven into psychological defenses. The simple way of describing defense is that it is a place where we shut down or act out. This is human nature. I see a new construct for working this. It is about working unworked material like shame, anxiety, or body discomfort—that is our trauma residue—for forty percent of the time, and working with gratitude and appreciation for sixty percent of the time. To know that the heart's wisdom is always greater than the limited bandwidth of defense.

"Be kind, everyone is fighting a great battle." A sign in a convenience store. What if we are all old souls wanting to find our way to the light? What if the rage and the despair we carry is miniscule in relation to our compassion and loving kindness? I believe we are on the cusp of a visionary time for the planet. I see the trajectory as moving from a place where we are culturally imploding and personally over-stimulated, depleted, to a place where we find trust and connection, trust in self, and trust in other. This phase shift, this threshold involves clearing our trauma residue and going out to talk with our neighbor. The daily practice is about cultivating a clear heart and peace in one's skin.

Individual history is implicit in the body. The life story is there in our voice, our posture, our aches and pains, the way we "light up" when we are happy. To have influence on the future, is to go to the body experience in the here and now. Hence the protocols. The protocols are divided under four categories. Of course there is ongoing overlap. Things aren't neat and tidy. My suggestion is to use the headings as an entry point and to imagine them as four points on a spiral that keeps unfolding.

Just as there is light and darkness inside of us, there is light and darkness outside of us. 9/11 happened and it transformed the consciousness of culture. The dire deed gave birth to generosity, open-ended community, amazing grace, and love. We are here on this planet to be spiritually whole. Much of what happened after 9/11 was a spontaneous arising of the light. The other side of the tragedy was shock, loss, despondency, anger.

Processing traumatic devastation near the time of the event gives us access to the spiritual song that is within all of us. This song knows the life course and knows that resiliency is the truth. We are here to help our neighbor and to love. Part of how we can extend relief is by addressing in a physiological way (rather than words) the impact of emotional overwhelm. Doing protocols for self and alongside another person after traumatic events gives an opportunity to soothe the nervous system and say to ourselves "We can make it."

It can be a rhythmic process as we address what is challenging, clear by doing a protocol, and follow through with appreciation for self. Appreciation for self is not to be underestimated. It is the locus of power and esteem. This is the noticing that we are in our feeling body, staying connected to our internal process, working it and moving on. Appreciating our willingness to change is the lynchpin piece in establishing worthiness. Appreciation is the piece the brain needs to make a whole cloth out of experience.

For everyday material, as well as during extraordinary times, doing protocols is about self-regulating internal states. In our working through psychological patterns, we are making sense of our experience from a different angle and in the process self-soothing. This results in a new internal state, that is a self-experience, that needs to be stabilized with appreciative regard. The more appreciation we have for self and for change, the stronger our cohesion becomes (see *The Heartmath Solution* for documentation of this).

This appreciation encompasses both the old and the new. We appreciate our old coping mechanisms even if they caused us pain repeatedly, and we appreciate the new way of staying connected. The bridge between the old and the new is the understanding that in a defensive response, we were in a place of adapting to our circumstances using the resources we had available. Surprising and not so surprising, the old coping skills also give us comfort (talk to any addict about this). It is our familiar way of making sense of the world. So important that the old ways of being get acknowledged as we wire in the new. What gets honored is the process of change.

Shadow work is simply looking behind us to see what others see, and we have had a hard time feeling connected to, because it is usually outside our range of vision. In our shadow, we find old hurts, anger, disappointments, fears. All of these things we are not particularly fond of. This trauma residue is more influential than we might imagine. This unworked material is what informs darkness. This unworked material is also the place where we increase our capacity to love self, fill in our wounds with consciousness, and extend our empowerment.

I am grouping shadow and trauma together, which may seem odd, because shadow is a place that can be hard to name while trauma may be evident and known, although often it is not. They are both about some kind of contraction, either in terms of awareness or feelings. Shadow and trauma can be split off because we need to survive and the raw reality of circumstance can make it too hard to keep everything on board. Core beliefs get tucked away out of sight in the process.

Yet shadow and trauma also both speak to our strengths and our ability to make it through. In the process of claiming shadow or trauma we also get the chance to bring it forward—in the very same process as creativity or humor. Think of your favorite comedian. How much of what he/she says is outrageous and funny because they are daring to speak what we are afraid to? They take material that is normally split off, speak it out loud, and in doing so clear the tension around it. Same deal for us.

Throughout all of this the working assumption is that everything is connected. Say a person has just done the *Releasing Anger* protocol and feels more settled, more connected. My guess is that there will also be a correspondence with a lessening of a physical symptom that is present at this time. Symptoms will often hold the space for feelings that are not worked. What that looks like is that we have feelings that we may not even know are there, but that are nonetheless. It is as if each feeling actually takes up space in our cells until we feel it and release it. Until then, a backlog happens and the feelings get pushed into symptoms as a way to hold them until we can get to them. The symptoms are helpful in that they catch our attention because they are often loud and insistent. The problem is that we haven't fully had the code to decipher them. We address them medically, which is good, but as many people are finding out it is not quite sufficient.

The theme here is to go to the body for a loving coherence. Go to the body in a heightened time in order to work the physical alarm, as well as to find spiritual comfort. The heart is a storehouse of wisdom. Go to the body to work old, stubborn emotional traits that interfere with empowerment. Go to the body with any symptom and ask "What do you want me to feel?" Go to the body with gratitude to increase a loving self capacity and make change sustainable over time. Put the focus on the body so the energy flows. Let feelings pass through like a guest. Feeling the experience of the body opens us to songs of manifestation. The songs are what we are here for.

5.

Shadow Blessed By Light

What is your aspiration? What do you most want? Whatever it is, your shadow, when brought into the light, will help you get there. But first, how in the world do you know what your shadow is? Shadow is defined by conventional wisdom as the part of ourselves that we can't tell is there. Let me give some examples. The shadow of an accomplished, successful professional could be about unworthiness. The shadow of an angry person who displays road rage and yells at her kids could be about shame and vulnerability. The shadow of the cheerful neighbor who volunteers at all the church socials could be about despondency.

Most of us work pretty hard at developing a sense of ourselves and presenting it to the world. This picture is certainly part of the truth but it is like the difference between a two-dimensional photo and a hologram. One is flat and portrays accurately what is presented for the moment. The three-dimensional hologram on the other hand has enormous depth. That is where the shadow lives, in the depth of our being, waiting to be noticed and wanting to be seen as part of the whole.

Growing up it is the parent's job to see their child, to accurately notice who they are, and to give words to that noticing to the child. The child will incorporate this reflection as part of their identity. The wheel turns and it becomes our developmental job as adults to see all of who we are, including our shadow, so that our identity is inclusive including all that is, as contrasted to narrowly defined.

People often make it to therapy because they are stuck and

unhappy in their lives, and need someone to "see them," so that they can make other choices. Therapy is certainly one way to work shadow material, but there are others as well. Feedback from intimate relationships and friends is another way. The protocols provide access to feelings and information under the surface. Spiritual practices can be a fine way to further a deeper sense of self. It is less about which vehicle one uses and more about getting on the road, seeing what is there. At that point, the spirit of discovery can take over.

You may wonder, what is the usefulness of plumbing the depths in order to uncover something on the order of inadequacy, rage, or shame. In some ways, it is like a traditional fairy tale: going on a journey and encountering monsters of various forms, and having to find the wits to "defeat them." Think of Ulysses and all his trials before he could return home. What I am suggesting is less about doing battle with our shadow, and more about establishing an inquiring relationship with the shadow material.

Trauma residue, for most of us, is inevitable. It runs a continuum from dealing with a one-time car accident as an adult, to severe trauma sexually, emotionally, physically. The whole gamut is there.

When we have intolerable feelings, either with trauma residue, or with shadow material, we tend to do one of two things: either we bury them in the far resources of our psyche-body, or we project outward. As part of human nature, we so want the bad to be outside of us. If we are holding onto a lot of disturbing feelings, if we are overwhelmed, if our body hurts, we could be creating resonance with a pattern that limits us. To know, that we only harm self or other out of our unworked places. A pattern could be about enduring, making due, or perhaps be a pattern that makes another person to blame. The latter is a very different place from a straight-forward place of seeking accountability with other. It is complex, trying to figure out what is inside of us, what is a fair accounting outside of us, what we need to keep, and what we need to lose. It is not about conquering our shadow, rather, coming to it with a mindful consciousness, a request of highest good, a curiosity about its origin. Assume that distress is a code from spirit. If your heart is sure of this, anything, anything can be worked.

It is said in the trauma field that anyone who has experienced abuse also has depression, that there is a one-to-one correspondence as part of the picture. Independent of major trauma, how many of us with a mild trauma residue, also have some low-key depression going on in the background that flattens what we do. Anxiety and depression are signpost of our culture. How many people do you know who are stressed, anxious, blue, and/or taking medication? Okay, so this is what we have to work with; the danger is becoming habituated to it, and assuming that this is the life course. Resignation to a bleak day to day life is a lousy way to go.

What I am suggesting is to go to the body with protocols and use them as a way to work this material. Take ten minutes a day, be in connection with the body and with an intent that releases a feeling of being less than, that releases despair. Explore what your limiting beliefs are, explore patterns that reoccur for you, explore what it feels like to be comfortable in your body with a clear heart.

Remember someone who has been kind to you and how you carry that in your heart. This is your inheritance: to carry forward that kindness. As we make a commitment to move through our trauma residue, what happens is an enormous confidence in our ability to influence the good of a situation. This is our birthright. Shadow material is the gateway to what we are here for. It just needs to be understood for what it is—distress that wants to be claimed consciously, to be held in the light, to be released. Take heart, the bright goodness is your true nature. It holds all that you are, all feelings, all states of mind. It is the felt experience of wholeness making room for every feeling. That happens, and then we have free choice and a unified mind and body.

Key Protocols

Awakening Heartfulness
Beginning Again

Brain Splits and Wholeness
Loving Self No Matter What
Moving Through Intrusive Thoughts, Moving to Insight
Releasing Anger
Releasing Fear
Releasing Shame
Releasing the Old
Retooling the Divided Self

6.

The Loved Body

There is a story we can name about our life. There is also a parallel story, that has all the unexpressed feelings from the story of our life. These unexpressed feelings can go directly into symptoms, as a way to carry the story forward. When we connect those feelings with the present symptoms, the two parallel lines converge. There is insight into perhaps a limiting belief, and an energetic release in the body. We have hit paydirt. The body is truly aching to convey meaning.

I believe there is a story in most any symptom we have that persists. It is all about not taking the symptom as the whole story. It is the brightly colored thread that, if we follow, will lead us out of the woods to the clearing. The clearing is the place of revelation. We have in our story energetic resonances—like energy attracts like energy—which can act like a magnet, bringing experience to us, and interpreting events. If a person believes that their creativity is huge, but that they mess up in relationship, you can probably get a snapshot of what their life looks like without knowing them.

This is because the body expresses the unconscious. The body expresses limiting beliefs. The representation of this distress can be manifested as symptoms. The body expresses trauma residue as its own story until a new story is revealed. This does not mean we cause our symptoms. No, no, no. It is about being an interconnected, complex system where everything relates to everything else. If we feel "bad" and it is our "fault" because we have a symptom, that might be the limiting belief about another experience in our life that is getting transposed on the symptom.

The place about our "fault" is just the belief that needs to clear. We may have that belief in a number of situations and clearing it, clears it in other situations as well. The power is to see what is there and to see if it is connected to a limiting belief or an emotionally constricted pattern. This is about giving more words to the internal experience.

It is interesting that the four releasing protocols are key in this section as well: *Releasing Anger, Releasing Fear, Releasing Shame, Releasing the Old.* Let's look at anger for a moment. A useful and important tool if it is conscious and skillful. The problem is that anger might actually be unconscious rage that contributes to symptoms. Unconscious means just that, that it is not available to cognitive perception.

Think of the barrier of the unconscious as a heavy lead door that is not framed in well, so what is behind the door seeps out in the cracks around the frame. The process of making material that is unconscious conscious is about opening the lead door to find a well made screen that is a boundary between the unconscious and conscious, and that lets air move freely back and forth. What a relief, the pressure is off when there is access to the screen door.

The releasing of anger in the example named would be about the body acknowledging what is pent up and allowing it to move through. What is left is a conscious anger that is articulate and as it is expressed, it is also cleared. The model then is going to the body with an intent to work anger with a protocol, opening the lead door to find an intact sturdy screen, letting air move through, and noting if there is a diminishment with the symptoms as a result of going to the body.

The concern people have is that if they begin to work with a feeling, that it could be overwhelming. What is truly overwhelming are the effects of denial. The long term outcome of denial is far worse than the short term effect from working uncomfortable feelings. The fact is that we all have unconscious emotions. We have feelings that are uncomfortable to feel, so we put them in storage. Healing is about using a safe means to move the emotions from the unconscious, while acknowledging their existence. Symptoms point the way to unacknowledged feelings. This is the good news.

Does this mean that every symptom we have is tied to big, old, unconscious material? When is a cold just a cold? What I am particularly talking about are tough lingering symptoms and symptoms that resist standard medical intervention. In these places, it behooves us to trust the body's innate intelligence and drive for well being. There is a mystery here that is about our greatest good. The greatest good being the interweaving of our spirit, our symptoms, our history, our hopes and dreams. If we are not up to date with some part of that interweaving, we may get a strong message that says pay attention, there is suffering going on.

Consciously connecting and weaving the parts into the whole may not stop the progression of disease, or restore functionality to degenerative illness, but it may give a sustaining grace. It is about saying "I am here doing everything I can to be present this moment." It is about loving the body unconditionally, loving the body, loving self with whatever is going on.

What this looks like is assuming the body has a vast intelligence that has as its premise that we are an amazing interconnected being. We have a stubborn, painful symptom and we work it medically as well as from a psychological point of view. What develops from this is an appreciation of our complexity, an appreciation for our willingness to listen to the body in a new way, an appreciation for allowing change to flow through. This back and forth dialogue with the body makes way for insight. Insight and opening the heart make way for love. Love, as the saying goes, is what we are here for. This capacity to love self and love the body in the midst is the sustaining grace. Praise be.

Key Protocols

Five-Minute Shame Release
Five-Step Flow

Letting it Steep
Releasing Anger
Releasing Fear
Releasing Shame
Releasing the Old
Retooling the Divided Self
Returning to the Heart
Safe to Heal
Sexual Healing
Speaking One's Truth
Wake Up

7.

Help Is On The Way

The other title for this section could be Receiving Care. Natural and unnatural catastrophes do happen. Scientists are saying that extreme weather conditions are increasing. There is extreme violence in the world political situation. Not everywhere and yet it seems we know in some part of our being that we are linked by humanity to all parts of the world. So here we are. Relief workers and relief agencies do a mighty job. What needs to be included as part of the vision of help is addressing the emotional shock and overwhelm inherent in tragic upheavals. This can be done with gestural protocols. It is important to note that I am not talking about verbal processing, which truly can be done later (and is actually better to be done later). What I am interested in is how a person moves from a place of victimization in regards to their circumstance, to a place of resource, resiliency, and relationship.

The protocols work to increase brain capacity especially under duress. They support whole brain functioning. When there is overwhelming trauma the brain can lateralize, that is, the two hemispheres stop talking to each other, as contrasted to synchrony, where there is a maximum flow of information between the two hemispheres. What this looks like is a person could be disoriented, dazed, disconnected because of the trauma. The gestural protocols I am suggesting would in many ways ameliorate the intensity of the symptoms, so what you could see is a very sad person, who is oriented and present.

I am particularly interested in affective neuroscience and the research that now recognizes that the brain reshapes itself according to experience. This neuroplasticity means that as we change the capacity in the brain, we also change our capacity to access resource. I believe it is all about resource. A basic truth for me is that we all do the best we can depending on the resource we have. We grow our brain by working our pain, and the brain grows with us. We grow by working our pain, and our compassion widens. Perhaps there is no finer resource than compassion for self and other. And for the compassion to come forward, extreme emotional arousal needs to be lessened.

The ability to regulate charged feeling in the midst can help to ease much suffering. Needless to say, loss and destruction can engender great despondency. By returning to the resource in the body, returning to compassion, the person can find a means to keep on going while transmuting the hopelessness.

This for some situations is a daily task. Similarly, the feelings of victimization in a catastrophic situation can be huge. Accessing internal resource can be a direct antidote to the collapse that occurs with feelings of victimization.

This is about helping a person return to functionality, while simultaneously providing tools to soothe and calm. The gestural protocols that I have developed are tools to regain resiliency and with that resiliency to further community, so that one neighbor can more easily help another neighbor. The intactness of one individual builds community. The intactness of many individuals rebuilds the community. With tools to balance the brain and steady the heart, there is light in the day and a possibility of tomorrow.

Key Protocols

Black Holes, Hopelessness, and Getting Back Home
Emotional First Aid
Forward Flow
Letting Out the Steam on Powerful Feelings
Releasing Survivor's Guilt

Resource in a Crisis
Self-Soothing in Troubled Times
Songs of the Heart
Sun and the Moon First Aid
Three-Step Flow
When the World Is Too Much

8.

The Everyday Luminous Self

This section is about bringing it all together. Life happens and we are in the midst of a terrifying circumstance. As part of the gestalt, we respond with energy medicine, with energetic mudras as a way to metabolize physiological alarm. And we carry on from there. Or we might have chronic physical complaints that elude treatment. We attend to them with the mind/body/heart interface of the protocols and find feelings that are just waiting to be felt, so that they can move through. The suffering from the symptoms is lessened because of the emotional connection. We identify our conditioned places of trauma residue, we bring light/consciousness to our shadow, we take refuge in relating to the body rather than disassociating from it.

This healing is a daily practice. We address the splits we have in mind, body, or spirit. We address the next layer and the layer after that. I believe we do that with heart-centered practices that stay connected to body states. I believe we do that with a mindful attunement to self. We heal our pain by attending to our everyday experiences and the patterns that hold them. The benchmark has been transformed to a standard of well-being and empowerment. There is the recognition of the places where we are powerless, and there is the assurance of being able to move mountains with our own material that is worked through.

This is it, this is the luminous everyday self. It is all about awakening the heart and allowing change to manifest. I envision the heart as the ancient alchemical vessel that changes lead into gold. If we are troubled, the heart holds us and heals. It is a vessel we bring our cares and concerns to. It is here we generate loving kindness towards self no matter what. It is here we transmute our suffering, our intolerable feelings into wisdom. It is here we generate compassion.

The heart is both a container and a pump. It contains our emotions and establishes flow to all parts of the body. If all is going well, there is both flow and steadiness. There is the experience of what opens the heart—joy, compassion, love for others—and there is the experience of what closes the heart—numbness, fear, hatred, negativity. Using gestures of the heart is about returning to the awareness of the heart on a daily basis, making the commitment to connect with the loving wisdom that is within no matter how discouraged with life, returning to this receptive resting position with the heart.

Connecting with the heart can be both hands on the heart, or crossing the hands in *Heart Blessing,* which in sign language is the symbol for "hug", as a way to direct our attention. Or connecting the heart and any other part of the body, as a way to further blood flow and contact between these two points. By putting awareness on the heart, physically and emotionally, in times of upheaval we call on a greater wholeness. This is about turning it around at the heart. In fact, this is what strengthens resiliency—to be "downhearted" and to keep faith and trust in one's capacity to go the distance. Working both ends: the places where we feel demoralized and depleted as well as the places where there is a fine esteem. This working with the light and dark of our experience extends our coherence, our innate capacity of resource, exponentially.

As a culture, we need to embody heartfulness because not doing so is killing us like none other. The antidote is going to the heart with your personal practice, with both hands on the heart, with asking if what you are doing in your life is in harmony with your deep true self. Simple and also requiring courage to feel all that is there (not just cognitively naming what is there) and to move one's life in accord with that knowing. If we are peaceful in our heart, it radiates out to all cells. This is what lights the way. The practice is about the neurological wiring in, that is repetition, of a loving appreciation of self. The loving appreciation of self spontaneously extends out to family, friends, community, strangers. We live up to the dream of a heart awakened to its true nature.

Key Protocols

Deepening the Capacity for Joy
Full Unreserved Resource
Furthering an Intent
Give-Away
Going the Distance With an Intent
Greeting the World with Appreciation
Heart's Protection
Making Room for Regard
Remembering the True Self
Space That Holds All That You Are
Voice and Vision

Part III.

Protocols for Healing

Key to the Protocols

Addictions
◆ Returning to the Heart

Anger, Rage
◆ Emotional First Aid
◆ Letting Out the Steam on Powerful Feelings
◆ Releasing Anger
◆ Sun and the Moon First Aid

Anxiety
◆ Emotional First Aid
◆ Forward Flow
◆ Returning to the Heart
◆ Sun and the Moon First Aid

Attachment
◆ Beginning Again

Comfort
◆ Five-Step Flow
◆ Safe to Heal
◆ Self-Soothing in Troubled Times
◆ Sun and the Moon First Aid

Creativity
◆ Full Unreserved Resource
◆ Voice and Vision

Depression
◆ Black Holes, Hopelessness, and Getting Back Home
◆ Emotional First Aid
◆ Resource in a Crisis
◆ Sun and the Moon First Aid

Distress
◆ Black Holes, Hopelessness, and Getting Back Home
◆ Emotional First Aid
◆ Self-Soothing in Troubled Times
◆ Space That Holds All You Are
◆ Sun and the Moon First Aid
◆ When the World Is Too Much

Energy Flow
◆ Emotional First Aid
◆ Five-Step Flow
◆ Forward Flow
◆ Sun and the Moon First Aid
◆ Three-Step Flow

Fear, Terror
◆ Emotional First Aid
◆ Letting Out the Steam on Powerful Feelings
◆ Releasing Fear
◆ Sun and the Moon First Aid

Gratitude
◆ Give-Away
◆ Greeting the World With Appreciation
◆ Heart's Protection: Openness and Gratitude

Grief
◆ Releasing the Old
◆ Songs of the Heart

Guilt, Regret
◆ Loving Self No Matter What
◆ Releasing the Old
◆ Space That Holds All You Are

Insight
◆ Moving Through Intrusive Thoughts, Moving to Insight
◆ Speaking One's Truth
◆ Voice and Vision

Insomnia
◆ Five-Step Flow

Intent
◆ Forward Flow
◆ Furthering an Intent
◆ Going the Distance with an Intent
◆ Letting It Steep
◆ Three-Step Flow

Intrusive Thought
◆ Moving Through Intrusive Thoughts, Moving to Insight

Letting Go
◆ Awakening Heartfulness: A Practice of Self-Forgiveness
◆ Releasing Anger
◆ Releasing Fear
◆ Releasing Shame
◆ Releasing the Old

Opening the Heart to Happiness
◆ Deepening the Capacity for Joy
◆ Heart's Protection: Openness and Gratitude

Positive Regard for Self
◆ Deepening the Capacity for Joy
◆ Full Unreserved Resource
◆ Making Room for Regard
◆ Remembering True Self

Releasing Trauma
◆ Resource in a Crisis
◆ Returning to the Heart
◆ Safe to Heal

Self-compassion, Self-forgiveness
◆ Awakening Heartfulness: A Practice of Self-Forgiveness
◆ Loving Self No Matter What
◆ Remembering True Self
◆ Returning to the Heart
◆ Safe to Heal

Separation from True Self
◆ Brain Splits and Wholeness
◆ Loving Self No Matter What
◆ Releasing Shame
◆ Retooling the Divided Self

Sexual Healing
◆ Sexual Healing

Shame
◆ Five-Minute Shame Release
◆ Letting Out the Steam on Powerful Feelings
◆ Releasing Shame

Survivor's Guilt
◆ Releasing Survivor's Guilt

Trance State
◆ Emotional First Aid
◆ Resource in a Crisis
◆ Sun and the Moon First Aid
◆ Wake Up

Awakening Heartfulness: A Practice of Self-Forgiveness

Purpose

♦ Forgiveness towards self is a linchpin piece in claiming whole-ness. Its counterpoint, being unforgiving towards self, is not to be underestimated in terms of the harm that it can cause with hold-ing in the muscles, the fascia, perhaps even the organs that gov-ern the body. Returning to self-forgiveness can be like returning to the awareness of the breath, something that we do over and over again.

Two-Minute Simple Balance

1. Drink water.

2. Hook up the hemispheres of the brain with *Heart Blessing*. With hands crossed over the chest, alternate tapping with each hand.

3. Rest in the heart for a moment with both hands on the heart.

Procedure

1. In Buddhism, the traditional loving kindness practice begins with an intent for oneself: May I be free of suffering. Here the intent for self is: I forgive myself for any harm I have done to self or other at any time.

Step 3

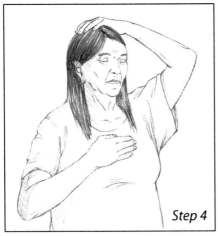

Step 4

2. Place one hand on the heart and one hand on the chin (CV 24) for two minutes.

3. *Forehead-Heart Hold:* Hold one hand on the forehead covering the third eye and one hand on the heart for two minutes.

4. *Crown-Heart Hold:* Hold one hand on the crown and one hand on the heart for two minutes.

5. Place one hand on the heart and one hand on the throat for two minutes.

6. Imagine a compassionate being of light in your heart center, radiating forgiveness in the form of a pink light that infuses your being with the essence of loving kindness.

Check-In

◆ Notice the sensations in your body. Notice if any feelings have changed and, if so, how.

Notes

◆ A self-forgiveness practice can be the ground of all other work. It is like chipping away layers of paint on an old house, getting to the bare wood. The bare wood, once freed of the residue of years, is ready to shine.

◆ A variation on the Tibetan Buddhist practice of tonglen is using it as a forgiveness practice for others. It works like this: taking in any harm someone else has done to you, transforming it in the fire of the heart, and breathing out a deep forgiveness. Doing this for several breaths.

Beginning Again

This protocol needs another person or therapist to facilitate. It is done in silence; all processing is done afterwards.

Purpose

♦ To establish neurological connection when a person has not been able to keep an internal representation of someone they care about and thus self-soothe.

♦ To ease shame, guilt, and anxiety at a core level.

♦ To help repair poor early attachment because of neglect.

Two-Minute Simple Balance

1. Drink water.

2. Hook up the hemispheres of the brain with *Heart Blessing*. With hands crossed over the chest, alternate tapping with each hand.

3. Rest in the heart for a moment with both hands on the heart.

Procedure

1. The person receiving the work keeps in mind and body the core issue of what he or she is working on (which is called being "in state") while the other person slowly draws a sideways figure-8 for two minutes in front of them with two fingers. The person receiving the work tracks the fingers with the eyes, without moving the head, while keeping both hands on the heart.

2. The person facilitating the work looks at the person receiving the work with unconditional care and regard. The person receiving the work looks at the other person's left eye (the person facilitating the work should not wear glasses). Do this for approximately two minutes.

3. *Eyelid Sweep:* With an index finger at the inner corner of each eye, gently pull the fingers over each eyelid and around back of the earlobes. Then begin again. Do this 10 to 20 times.

Step 4

4. *Head-Heart Hold:* Hold one hand at the back of your head and one hand on your heart for two minutes.

5. Wiggle your toes.

Check-In

◆ Notice the sensations in your body. Notice if any feelings have changed and, if so, how.

Note

◆ This protocol combines four things: an experiential place of charged material, a holding environment where there is care and regard, self-soothing with the *Eyelid Sweep,* and body integration with the *Head-Heart Hold.*

Black Holes, Hopelessness, and Getting Back Home

Purpose

- ◆ To access body wisdom in times of internal turmoil.
- ◆ To help actualize the clear, true self.

Two-Minute Simple Balance

1. Drink water.

2. Hook up the hemispheres of the brain with *Heart Blessing.* With hands crossed over the chest, alternate tapping with each hand.

3. Rest in the heart for a moment with both hands on the heart.

Procedure

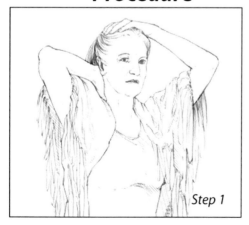

Step 1

1. *Middle-Ground Mudra:* Hold one hand on the crown and one hand on the back of the head for two minutes.

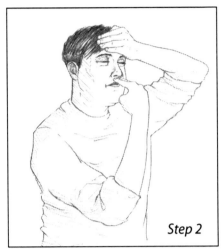

Step 2

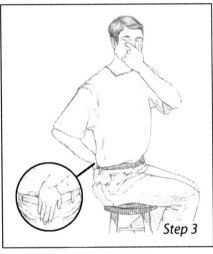

Step 3

2. *Basic Relief:* Hold one hand on the forehead and one hand beneath the nose (at GV26) for two minutes.

3. *Solid Ground:* With one hand, massage under the eyes (at St2) with the thumb and index finger, while holding the other hand on the sacrum for two minutes.

4. Name two intents for yourself, one having to do with self-soothing and one with the larger view in regards to your healing.

5. Imagine your body is an oak tree. Imagine the intents as underground, the root system for this large tree of life. Breathe the intents up from the roots, through the trunk, and with the exhale, out to the branches. Do this several times.

6. *Eye Opener:* Make a sideways figure-8 eye movement (eyes upper right, lower right, upper left, lower left, and back to upper right) while holding hands on the heart for one minute.

7. Write down at least one learning (intuitive insight) that is important to carry forward.

Check-In

◆ Notice the sensations in your body. Notice if any feelings have changed and, if so, how.

Brain Splits and Wholeness

Purpose

- To weave together experiences that have been disconnected from and the present moment, as well as weave together remembered experiences so there can be, over time, words that make it a story.

Two-Minute Simple Balance

1. Drink water.

2. Hook up the hemispheres of the brain with *Heart Blessing.* With hands crossed over the chest, alternate tapping with each hand.

3. Rest in the heart for a moment with both hands on the heart.

Procedure

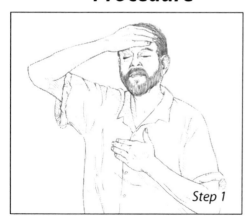

Step 1

1. *Forehead-Heart Hold:* Hold one hand on the forehead covering the third eye and one hand on the heart for two minutes, setting an intention for the brain to be gently pulsing with vital energy, neuropathways open.

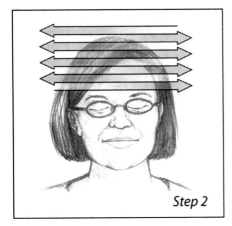

Step 2

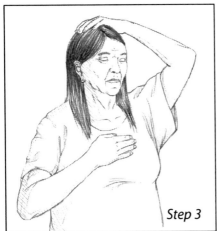

Step 3

2. *Gold-White Weave:* Imagine gold light going from the right hemisphere to the left hemisphere of your brain; at the same time imagine white light going from the left hemisphere to the right hemisphere, the golden white light overlapping, forming a radiant weave of light, filling the entire brain.

3. *Crown-Heart Hold:* Hold one hand on the crown and one hand on the heart for two minutes. This connects our higher knowing with the wisdom of the heart.

4. *Wise Brain Mudra:* Hold one hand on the forehead and one hand on the crown for two minutes.

5. *Eye Opener:* Make a sideways figure-8 eye movement (eyes moving upper right, lower right, upper left, lower left, and back to upper right) while holding hands on the heart for one minute.

6. *Eyelid Sweep:* Starting with an index finger at the inner corner of each eye, gently pull the fingers over each eyelid, across the temple, and around the back of the earlobes. Then start over again. Do this 10 to 20 times.

Check-In

◆ Notice the sensations in your body. Notice if any feelings have changed and, if so, how.

Deepening the Capacity for Joy

Purpose

♦ To increase the ability to hold happiness. This is for many people a developed skill just like holding difficult feelings is something that needs to be cultivated.

Two-Minute Simple Balance

1. Drink water.

2. Hook up the hemispheres of the brain with *Heart Blessing.* With hands crossed over the chest, alternate tapping with each hand.

3. Rest in the heart for a moment with both hands on the heart.

Procedure

Step 2

1. Set an intent to let joy flow, to be open in heart and body.

2. *Spacious Heart Breath:* Breathe into the heart center and, with the breath, trace an infinity symbol (a sideways figure-8) and breathe out the heart center. Do this for six breaths.

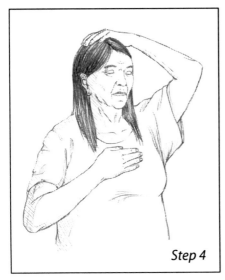

Step 4

Step 5

3. Hold one hand on the heart and one hand two inches below the navel for two minutes. This gesture encourages a soft belly and an open heart.

4. *Crown-Heart Hold:* With eyes closed, hold one hand on the crown and one hand on the heart for two minutes.

5. *Forehead-Heart Hold:* Hold one hand on the forehead covering the third eye and one hand on the heart for two minutes.

6. Return to holding both hands on the heart, feeling the rising and falling of your chest.

Check-In

♦ Notice the sensations in your body. Notice if any feelings have changed and, if so, how.

Emotional First Aid

Purpose
◆ To ease intense anger, anxiety, or distress.

Two-Minute Simple Balance

1. Drink water.

2. Hook up the hemispheres of the brain with *Heart Blessing.* With hands crossed over the chest, alternate tapping with each hand.

3. Rest in the heart for a moment with both hands on the heart.

Procedure

Step 2

1. *Back Again:* Tap or hold the thymus (at the second rib on the sternum) with one hand while the other hand taps or holds the chin for two minutes.

2. *Basic Relief:* Hold one hand on the forehead and one hand beneath the nose (at GV26) for two minutes.

Step 4

3. *Eyelid Sweep:* Starting with an index finger at the inner corner of each eye, gently pull the fingers over each eyelid, across the temple, and around the back of the earlobes. Then start over again. Do this 10 to 20 times.

4. *Brain Flow Mudra:* Hold one hand on the forehead and one hand on the back of the head for two minutes with the intention to convert anxiety into beneficial action.

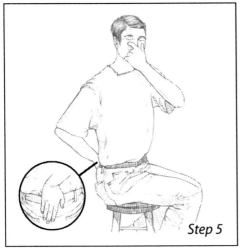

Step 5

5. *Solid Ground:* With one hand, massage under the eyes (at St2) with the thumb and index finger while the other hand is on the sacrum for two minutes.

Check-In

◆ Notice the sensations in your body. Notice if any feelings have changed and, if so, how.

Five-Minute Shame Release

Purpose

♦ To restore harmony in the body. Shame erodes esteem, cohesion, and perception. This protocol uses the first three steps of *Emotional First Aid* to re-establish confidence by metabolizing shame.

Two-Minute Simple Balance

1. Drink water.

2. Hook up the hemispheres of the brain with *Heart Blessing*. With hands crossed over the chest, alternate tapping with each hand.

3. Rest in the heart for a moment with both hands on the heart.

Procedure

Step 1

1. *Back Again:* Tap or hold the thymus (at the second rib on the sternum) with one hand while the other taps or holds the chin for two minutes.

Step 2

2. *Basic Relief:* Hold one hand on the forehead and one hand beneath the nose (at GV26) for two minutes.

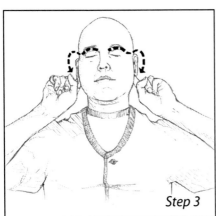

Step 3

3. *Eyelid Sweep:* Starting with an index finger at the corner of each eye, gently pull the fingers over each eyelid, across the temple, and around the back of the earlobes. Then start over again. Do this 10 to 20 times.

Check-In

◆ Notice the sensations in your body. Notice if any feelings have changed and, if so, how.

Five-Step Flow

Purpose

- ◆ To access full body awareness, that is, facilitate being in the body.
- ◆ To promote insight and to move that understanding through the body.
- ◆ To facilitate energy flow in the spinal cord while centering heart energy.
- ◆ To help move stuck energy.

Two-Minute Simple Balance

1. Drink water.

2. Hook up the hemispheres of the brain with *Heart Blessing.* With hands crossed over the chest, alternate tapping with each hand.

3. Rest in the heart for a moment with both hands on the heart.

Procedure

Step 1

1. *Brain Flow Mudra:* Hold one hand on the back of the head and one hand on the forehead for two minutes.

Step 2

2. *Head-Heart Hold:* Hold one hand on the back of the head and one hand on the heart for two minutes.

3. *Double-Hands Heart Hold:* Hold both hands on the heart for two minutes.

4. Hold one hand on the heart and one hand two inches below the navel for two minutes. This gesture encourages a soft belly and an open heart.

5. Hold one hand two inches below the naval and one hand on the sacrum for two minutes.

Check-In

◆ Notice the sensations in your body. Notice if any feelings have changed and, if so, how.

Note

◆ This protocol can also ease insomnia by letting the body settle in.

Forward Flow

Purpose

◆ To set an intention in heart and body for the highest good for oneself and for the situation that one is in. This protocol can also be used for a particular intention. It is about establishing a deep harmony with one's vision.

Two-Minute Simple Balance

1. Drink water.

2. Hook up the hemispheres of the brain with *Heart Blessing*. With hands crossed over the chest, alternate tapping with each hand.

3. Rest in the heart for a moment with both hands on the heart.

Procedure

1. *Crown-Heart Hold:* With eyes closed, hold one hand on the crown and one hand on the heart for two minutes.

2. Hold one hand on the heart and one hand on the sacrum for two minutes.

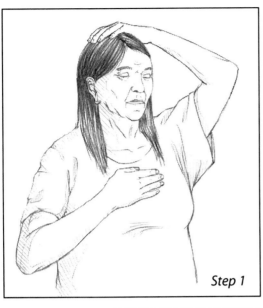

Step 1

Step 4

3. *Forehead-Heart Hold:* Hold one hand on the forehead covering the third eye and one hand on the heart for two minutes.

4. *Brain Flow Mudra:* Hold one hand on the back of the head and one hand on the forehead for two minutes.

5. Hold one hand on the back of the head and one hand below the navel for two minutes.

Check-In

◆ Notice the sensations in your body. Notice if any feelings have changed and, if so, how.

Full Unreserved Resource

Purpose

◆ To build in self-worth as a way to fully actualize self and further creativity.

Two-Minute Simple Balance

1. Drink water.

2. Hook up the hemispheres of the brain with *Heart Blessing*. With hands crossed over the chest, alternate tapping with each hand.

3. Rest in the heart for a moment with both hands on the heart.

Procedure

Step 1

1. *Eye Opener:* Make a sideways figure-8 eye movement (eyes upper right, lower right, upper left, lower left, and back to upper right) while holding hands on the heart for one minute.

2. *Head-Heart Hold:* Hold one hand on the back of the head and one hand on the heart with an intent to convert any anxiety into beneficial action for two minutes.

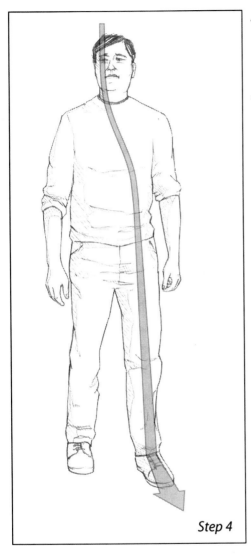

Step 4

3. Hold one hand on the sacrum and one hand on the chin for two minutes.

4. *Green Means Go:* Visualize healing green light coming into the right hemisphere of your brain with the inhale, the green light picking up any trauma residue, traveling to the heart, continuing to pick up any trauma residue, and on the exhale going down your left leg and out the sole of your left foot. Do this five to 10 times.

5. *Brain Flow Mudra:* Hold one hand on the forehead and one hand on the back of the head for two minutes.

6. *Gold-White Weave:* Imagine gold light going from the right hemisphere to the left hemisphere of your brain, at the same time imagining white light going from the left hemisphere to the right hemisphere, the golden white light overlapping, forming a radiant weave of light, filling the entire brain.

Check-In

◆ Notice the sensations in your body. Notice if any feelings have changed and, if so, how.

Furthering an Intent

Purpose

◆ Intents are one of the most powerful tools we have. This protocol is about naming an intent for oneself and bringing that focused energy to each of the energy gestures below.

Two-Minute Simple Balance

1. Drink water.

2. Hook up the hemispheres of the brain with *Heart Blessing*. With hands crossed over the chest, alternate tapping with each hand.

3. Rest in the heart for a moment with both hands on the heart.

Procedure

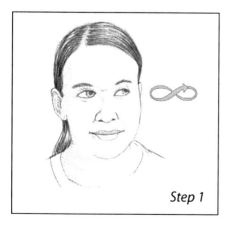

Step 1

1. *Eye Opener:* Make a sideways figure-8 eye movement (eyes upper right, lower right, upper left, lower left, and back to upper right) while holding hands on the heart for one minute.

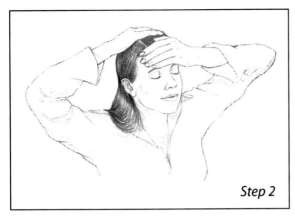

Step 2

2. *Wise Brain Mudra:* Hold one hand on the forehead and one hand on the crown for two minutes.

Step 3

3. *Brain Flow Mudra:* Hold one hand on the forehead and one hand on the back of the head for two minutes.

4. *Head-Heart Hold:* Hold one hand on the back of the head and one hand on the heart for two minutes.

5. Repeat *Eye Opener* for one minute.

Check-In

◆ Notice the sensations in your body. Notice if any feelings have changed and, if so, how.

Give-Away

Purpose

◆ This exercise is similar to the American Indian tradition of pot latch where one would bring something of value to give away to the community. One's wealth was measured by one's generosity. This meditation is about generosity of the heart and extending it to the world.

Two-Minute Simple Balance

1. Drink water.

2. Hook up the hemispheres of the brain with *Heart Blessing*. With hands crossed over the chest, alternate tapping with each hand.

3. Rest in the heart for a moment with both hands on the heart.

Procedure

1. Sit quietly with yourself, taking full deep breaths.

2. Let your heart be as open as the blue sky.

3. Name the things in your life that you are thankful for.

4. With one hand moving upward from the center of the sternum, feather out gratitude from the heart, ending in an open palm in front of you. Do this one hand after another.

5. Take the gladness in your heart and give it away.

6. Take the affection in your heart and give it to the earth.

7. Take your gratitude and give it to the stars.

Check-In

◆ Notice the sensations in your body. Notice if any feelings have changed and, if so, how.

Going the Distance With an Intent

Purpose

◆ To name an intent for oneself and to do the protocol for 40 days. The repetition, along with the image of the intent actualized, is a powerful way to unfold a new way of being in the world.

Two-Minute Simple Balance

1. Drink water.

2. Hook up the hemispheres of the brain with *Heart Blessing*. With hands crossed over the chest, alternate tapping with each hand.

3. Rest in the heart for a moment with both hands on the heart.

Procedure

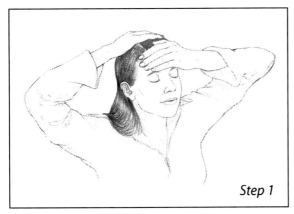

Step 1

1. *Laser Like:* Do *Wise Brain Mudra* (one hand on the forehead, one hand on the crown) for one minute followed by *Brain Flow Mudra* (one hand on the forehead, one hand on the back of the head) for two minutes. While holding, repeat the intent internally and visualize it accomplished.

Step 1

Step 2

2. *Head-Heart Hold:* Hold one hand on the back of the head and one hand on the heart for two minutes.

Check-In

◆ Notice the sensations in your body. Notice if any feelings have changed and, if so, how.

Greeting the World With Appreciation

Purpose

- ◆ To open our heart to others as a way to be in the world.
- ◆ To wish strangers well as a manifestation of our true self.
- ◆ To know that our happiness is dependent on the well-being of the world.

Two-Minute Simple Balance

1. Drink water.

2. Hook up the hemispheres of the brain with *Heart Blessing*. With hands crossed over the chest, alternate tapping with each hand.

3. Rest in the heart for a moment with both hands on the heart.

Procedure

1. *Going for Gold:* Place one hand under the collar bone (which corresponds to the thymus) and one hand on the heart for two minutes, and then both hands on the heart for two minutes.

2. Practice remembering the following words or any others that your heart speaks as you notice others in the grocery store, on the street, driving in your car or riding on the bus.

   "May you be filled with loving kindness."

   "May I be filled with loving kindness."

   "May we all be filled with loving kindness."

   "May all my actions benefit others."

Check-In

♦ Notice the sensations in your body. Notice if any feelings have changed and, if so, how.

Heart's Protection: Openness and Gratitude

Purpose

◆ To truthfully recognize the goodness in one's life.
◆ To see the big picture and take note.
◆ To strengthen the feeling of belonging.

Two-Minute Simple Balance

1. Drink water.

2. Hook up the hemispheres of the brain with *Heart Blessing*. With hands crossed over the chest, alternate tapping with each hand.

3. Rest in the heart for a moment with both hands on the heart.

Procedure

1. *Wise Brain Mudra:* Hold one hand on the forehead and one hand on the crown for two minutes.

2. *Going for Gold:* Place one hand under the collar bone (which corresponds to the thymus) and one hand on the heart for two minutes, and then both hands on the heart for two minutes.

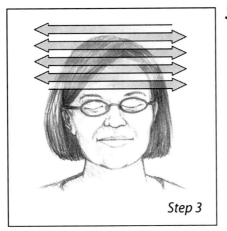

Step 3

3. *Gold-White Weave:* Imagine gold light going from the right hemisphere of your brain to the left hemisphere, at the same time imagining white light going from the left hemisphere to the right, the golden white light overlapping, forming a radiant weave of light, filling the entire brain.

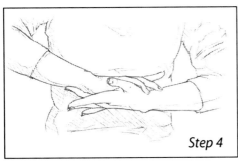

Step 4

4. *Gate to Peace:* Fold your forearms in front of your chest, and then slide your arms out until your palms are on top of each other. Alternate tapping with the middle finger just below the wrist crease for one minute. This provides bilateral stimulation of the brain while connecting with the pericardium meridian, which governs the heart.

5. As a seal to this practice, place both hands on the heart, remembering your true self: large, luminous, belonging to the world. There is the metaphor that awakening to our original nature, blue sky is everywhere. May we be fearless in the experience of blessing.

Check-In

◆ Notice the sensations in your body. Notice if any feelings have changed and, if so, how.

Letting It Steep

Purpose

- ◆ To strengthen an intent in the body.
- ◆ To stabilize openness, particularly during a time of quickened awareness.
- ◆ To be with what is going on in the body in order to help it metabolize and release.

Two-Minute Simple Balance

1. Drink water.

2. Hook up the hemispheres of the brain with *Heart Blessing.* With hands crossed over the chest, alternate tapping with each hand.

3. Rest in the heart for a moment with both hands on the heart.

Procedure

1. Hold one hand on the crown and one hand on the sacrum, breathing in the awareness of the body experience. Do this for several minutes.

2. Hold one hand on the sacrum and one hand on the heart for two minutes.

3. Hold one hand on the heart and one hand on the solar plexus, midway between your navel and the base of your sternum, for two minutes.

4. Hold one hand on the solar plexus and one hand on the throat for two minutes.

5. Read these sentences to yourself or say them aloud: May I live in ease and well-being. May all beings live in ease and well-being.

Check-In

♦ Notice the sensations in your body. Notice if any feelings have changed and, if so, how.

Letting Out the Steam on Powerful Feelings

Purpose

◆ To work with feelings that feel enormous, like terror, rage, or shame.

Two-Minute Simple Balance

1. Drink water.

2. Hook up the hemispheres of the brain with *Heart Blessing*. With hands crossed over the chest, alternate tapping with each hand.

3. Rest in the heart for a moment with both hands on the heart.

Procedure

1. *Express and Soothe:* Feather (tap) from the middle to the top of the sternum and release through the mouth with a strong exhale, alternating with *Heart Glide* (one hand after another gliding down over the heart).

2. *Forehead-Heart Hold:* Hold one hand on the forehead and one hand on the heart for two minutes.

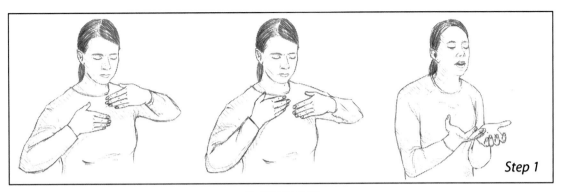

Step 1

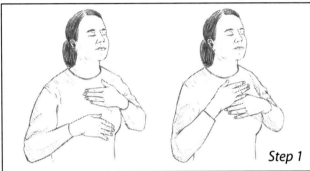

Step 1

3. *Spacious Heart Breath:* Breathe into the heart center and, with the breath, trace an infinity symbol (a sideways figure-8) and breathe out the heart center. Do this for six breaths.

4. *Synapse to Synapse:* With one hand, massage either side of the sternum at the collarbone (at K27) while the other hand is on the heart for two minutes.

5. *Laser Like:* Do *Wise Brain Mudra* (one hand on the forehead, one hand on the crown) for one minute followed by *Brain Flow Mudra* (one hand on the forehead, one hand on the back of the head) for two minutes.

Check-In

◆ Notice the sensations in your body. Notice if any feelings have changed and, if so, how.

Loving Self No Matter What

Purpose
◆ To help heal the split from the authentic self.
◆ To access body knowledge that taps into a wise knowing.

Two-Minute Simple Balance

1. Drink water.

2. Hook up the hemispheres of the brain with *Heart Blessing*. With hands crossed over the chest, alternate tapping with each hand.

3. Rest in the heart for a moment with both hands on the heart.

Procedure
1. Name a particular incident where you have bad feelings about yourself or regret. Breathe in the pain of what happened, breathe out loving kindness. Do this for a couple of minutes.

2. Hold one hand on the chin and one hand on the heart for two minutes.

3. Hold one hand on the chin and one hand on the solar plexus (midway between the navel and the base of the sternum) for two minutes.

4. Hold one hand on the solar plexus and one hand on the crown for two minutes.

5. Close your eyes and place both hands over your heart. From there, ask your deeper knowing these questions:

"How does the larger context of my life connect with this incident?"

"If it is true that I have messed up, how can I repair in this moment?"

"What do I need to do to be loving toward myself in this moment?"

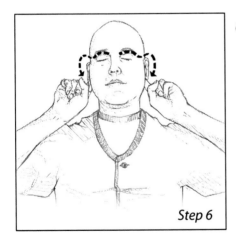

Step 6

6. *Eyelid Sweep:* Starting with an index finger at the inner corner of each eye, gently pull the fingers over each eyelid, across the temple, and around the back of the earlobes. Then start over again. Do this 10 to 20 times.

Check-In

◆ Notice the sensations in your body. Notice if any feelings have changed and, if so, how.

Making Room for Regard

Purpose

◆ To create a capacity for holding onto good feelings. Good feelings can be particularly ephemeral because it is as if they don't have a place to call their own in the body.

Two-Minute Simple Balance

1. Drink water.

2. Hook up the hemispheres of the brain with *Heart Blessing*. With hands crossed over the chest, alternate tapping with each hand.

3. Rest in the heart for a moment with both hands on the heart.

Procedure

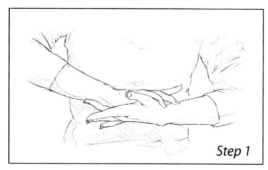

Step 1

1. *Gate to Peace:* Fold your forearms in front of your chest, and then slide your arms out until your palms are on top of each other. Alternate tapping with the middle finger just below the wrist crease for about one minute. This provides bilateral stimulation of the brain while connecting with the pericardium meridian, which governs the heart.

2. *Double-Hands Heart Hold:* Hold both hands on the heart for two minutes.

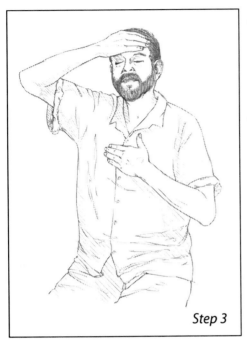

Step 3

3. *Forehead-Heart Hold:* Hold one hand on the forehead covering the third eye and one hand on the heart for two minutes.

4. Hold one hand on the heart and one hand on the sacrum for two minutes.

5. Massage your outer ears, opening the senses.

Check-In

♦ Notice the sensations in your body. Notice if any feelings have changed and, if so, how.

Moving Through Intrusive Thoughts, Moving to Insight

Purpose

◆ To clear obsessive thoughts.

◆ To help release memory charge from the body on an issue.

◆ To facilitate access to a larger understanding of the situation.

Two-Minute Simple Balance

1. Drink water.

2. Hook up the hemispheres of the brain with *Heart Blessing*. With hands crossed over the chest, alternate tapping with each hand.

3. Rest in the heart for a moment with both hands on the heart.

Procedure

Step 1

1. *Back Again:* Tap or hold the thymus (at the second rib on the sternum) with one hand while the other taps or holds the chin for two minutes.

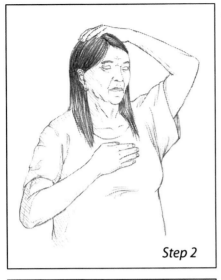

Step 2

2. *Crown-Heart Hold:* Hold one hand on the crown and one hand on the heart for two minutes. This connects our higher knowing with the wisdom of the heart.

3. *Head-Heart Hold:* Hold one hand on the back of the head and one hand on the heart for two minutes.

4. Hold one hand on the back of the head and one hand below the navel for two minutes.

Step 5

5. *Basic Relief:* Hold one hand on the forehead and one hand beneath the nose (at GV26) for two minutes.

Check-In

◆ Notice the sensations in your body. Notice if any feelings have changed and, if so, how.

Releasing Anger

Purpose

◆ To facilitate anger safely moving through the body, so there can be a clear heart. The key here is to acknowledge the anger, feel it, and move it through energetically. The structure of the protocol gives a form, so that anger can be responded to without being overwhelming or stored in the body.

Two-Minute Simple Balance

1. Drink water.

2. Hook up the hemispheres of the brain with *Heart Blessing*. With hands crossed over the chest, alternate tapping with each hand.

3. Rest in the heart for a moment with both hands on the heart.

Step 1

Procedure

1. *Forehead-Heart Hold:* Hold one hand on the forehead covering the third eye and one hand on the heart for two minutes

Step 2

2. *Brain Flow Mudra:* Hold one hand on the back of the head and one hand on the forehead for two minutes.

3. Place one hand on the back of the head and one hand below the navel for two minutes.

4. *Solid Ground:* With one hand, massage under the eyes (at St2) with the thumb and index finger while the other hand is on the sacrum for two minutes.

5. Place one hand under the nose (at GV 26) and the other hand on the sacrum for two minutes. (This is the Space Button in Brain Gym.)

6. Place one hand on the chin (at CV 24) and the other hand on the sacrum for two minutes.

Check-In

◆ Notice the sensations in your body. Notice if any feelings have changed and, if so, how.

Note

◆ If doing the protocol is not an option in the moment, anger can safely be transformed by imagining it coming to the heart and on the exhale leaving the heart, that is, on the inhale gathering the anger at the heart and, on the exhale, moving it out. Continue with rhythmic breathing at the heart center for several minutes. The heart welcomes the instruction to release.

Releasing Fear

Purpose

♦ Fear can paralyze. Fear can also be a catalyst. It often accompanies us when we are in the midst of major change. This protocol works with fear, so that we can convert the fear into a vision for where we want to go. This protocol serves as a general releasing protocol as well.

Two-Minute Simple Balance

1. Drink water.

2. Hook up the hemispheres of the brain with *Heart Blessing*. With hands crossed over the chest, alternate tapping with each hand.

3. Rest in the heart for a moment with both hands on the heart.

Procedure

Step 2

1. Place one hand below the navel and one hand at the forehead for two minutes.

2. *Synapse to Synapse:* With one hand, massage either side of the sternum at the collarbone (at K27) while the other hand is on the heart for two minutes.

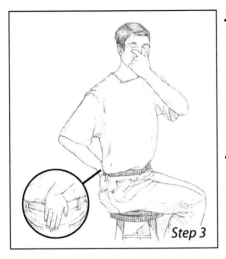

3. *Solid Ground:* Massage under the eyes (at St2) with the thumb and index finger while holding one hand at the sacrum for two minutes.

4. Hold one hand on the sacrum and one hand underneath the nose (GV 26) for two minutes. (This is the Space Button in Brain Gym.)

5. Hold one hand on the sacrum and one hand on the chin (CV 24) for two minutes.

Check-In

◆ Notice the sensations in your body. Notice if any feelings have changed and, if so, how.

Releasing Shame

Purpose

◆   To help dissolve the bonds of shame.

Two-Minute Simple Balance

1. Drink water.

2. Hook up the hemispheres of the brain with *Heart Blessing*. With hands crossed over the chest, alternate tapping with each hand.

3. Rest in the heart for a moment with both hands on the heart.

Procedure

1. Notice your body state. It is helpful for the feelings to be present for them to move through the body and release. Be with the shame in a safe way. If at any point it becomes overwhelming, softly tap the heart as a way to come back to the body.

Step 3

2. *Eye Opener:* Make a sideways figure-8 eye movement (eyes upper right, lower right, upper left, lower left, and back to upper right) while holding hands on the heart for one minute.

3. *Head-Heart Hold:* Hold one hand at the back of the head and one hand on the heart for two minutes.

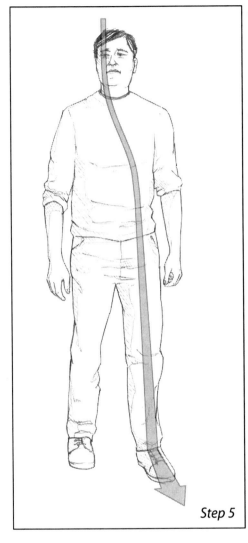

Step 5

4. *Back Again:* Tap or hold the thymus (at the second rib on the sternum) with one hand and, with the other hand, tap or hold the chin for two minutes.

5. *Green Means Go:* Visualize healing green light coming into the right hemisphere of your brain with the inhale, the green light picking up any trauma residue, traveling to the heart, continuing to pick up any trauma residue, and on the exhale going down your left leg and out the sole of your left foot. Do this five to 10 times.

6. *Brain Flow Mudra:* Hold one hand on the forehead and one hand on the back of the head for two minutes.

7. Read these sentences to yourself or say them aloud: May I enjoy the root of happiness. May all beings enjoy the root of happiness.

Check-In
◆ Notice the sensations in your body. Notice if any feelings have changed and, if so, how.

Notes
◆ It is helpful to do this practice every day for 10 days with as much consistency as possible to lessen the physiological conditioning around shame. It can also be done as a one-time response to deal with an acute feeling state of shame.
◆ If the shame is released, this will make the feelings underneath the shame more available.

Releasing Survivor's Guilt

Purpose

◆ To give clarity and understanding for surviving emotionally or physically in a situation where someone else did not.

Two-Minute Simple Balance

1. Drink water.

2. Hook up the hemispheres of the brain with *Heart Blessing*. With hands crossed over the chest, alternate tapping with each hand.

3. Rest in the heart for a moment with both hands on the heart.

Procedure

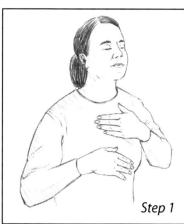

Step 1

1. *Heart Glide:* Glide one hand after another down over the heart.

2. *Brain Flow Mudra:* Hold one hand on the back of the head and one hand on the forehead for two minutes.

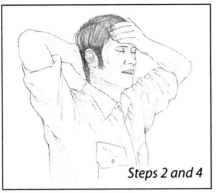

Steps 2 and 4

3. *Spacious Heart Breath:* Breathe into the heart center and, with the breath, trace an infinity symbol (a sideways figure-8) and breathe out the heart center. Do this for six breaths.

4. *Brain Flow Mudra:* Hold one hand on the back of the head and one hand on the forehead for two minutes.

Step 5

5. *Synapse to Synapse:* With one hand, massage either side of the sternum at the collarbone (at K27) while the other hand is on the heart for two minutes.

6. Write down at least one learning that is from the heart's wisdom.

Check-In

◆ Notice the sensations in your body. Notice if any feelings have changed and, if so, how.

Releasing the Old

Purpose

◆   To facilitate the letting go of that which no longer serves and to make way for the new.

Two-Minute Simple Balance

1. Drink water.

2. Hook up the hemispheres of the brain with *Heart Blessing*. With hands crossed over the chest, alternate tapping with each hand.

3. Rest in the heart for a moment with both hands on the heart.

Procedure

1. Massage your lower back at waist level to increase blood flow to that region. (If you have an injury there, just hold a hand on your lower back.)

Step 2

2. *Middle-Ground Mudra:* Hold one hand on the crown and one hand on the back of the head for two minutes.

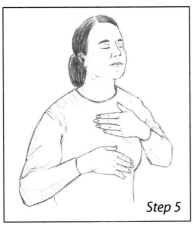

Step 5

3. Hold one hand on the back of the head and one hand below the navel for two minutes.

4. Hold one hand below the navel and one hand on the sacrum for two minutes.

5. *Heart Glide:* Glide one hand after the other down over the heart. If so inclined, you may wish to bless the old as it releases.

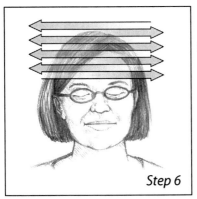

Step 6

6. *Gold-White Weave:* Imagine gold light going from the right hemisphere to the left hemisphere of your brain, at the same time imagining white light going from the left hemisphere to the right, the golden white light overlapping, forming a radiant weave of light, filling the entire brain.

Check-In

◆ Notice the sensations in your body. Notice if any feelings have changed and, if so, how.

Remembering True Self

Purpose
- ◆ To remember the basic goodness of one's heart.
- ◆ To remember the home ground of the true self.

Two-Minute Simple Balance

1. Drink water.

2. Hook up the hemispheres of the brain with *Heart Blessing*. With hands crossed over the chest, alternate tapping with each hand.

3. Rest in the heart for a moment with both hands on the heart.

Procedure

Step 1

1. *Forehead-Heart Hold:* Hold one hand on the forehead covering the third eye and one hand on the heart for two minutes, creating a circle of love by sending the intention of loving kindness to one's self in the past, loving kindness to one's self in the present, loving kindness to one's self in the future.

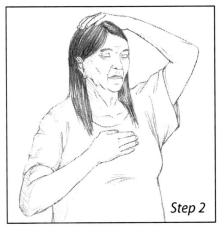
Step 2

2. *Crown-Heart Hold:* Hold one hand on the crown and one hand on the heart for two minutes. This connects our higher knowing with the wisdom of the heart.

3. *Wise Brain Mudra:* Hold one hand on the crown and one hand on the forehead for two minutes.

Step 4

4. *Spacious Heart Breath:* Breathe into the heart center and, with the breath, trace an infinity symbol (a sideways figure-8) and breathe out the heart center. Do this for six breaths.

Check-In

◆ Notice the sensations in your body. Notice if any feelings have changed and, if so, how.

Resource in a Crisis

Purpose

◆ To create strong neural circuitry in precarious emotional circumstances. It is all about cohesion when we are in the midst. Practically, this is about increasing blood flow to the brain, calming arousal, and connecting to the heart.

Two-Minute Simple Balance

1. Drink water.

2. Hook up the hemispheres of the brain with *Heart Blessing.* With hands crossed over the chest, alternate tapping with each hand.

3. Rest in the heart for a moment with both hands on the heart.

Procedure

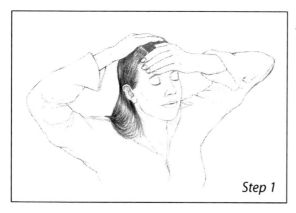

Step 1

1. *Wise Brain Mudra:* Hold one hand on the crown and one hand on the forehead for two minutes.

Step 2

2. *Brain Flow Mudra:* Hold one hand on the back of the head and one hand on the forehead for two minutes.

3. *Head-Heart Hold:* Hold one hand at the back of the head and one hand on the heart for two minutes.

Step 3

4. *Eyelid Sweep:* Starting with an index finger at the inner corner of each eye, gently pull the fingers over each eyelid, across the temple, and around the back of the earlobes. Then start over again. Do this 10 to 20 times.

5. Rest with both hands on the heart for two minutes.

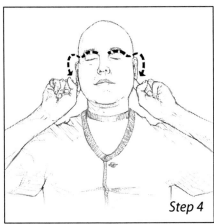

Step 4

Check-In

◆ Notice the sensations in your body. Notice if any feelings have changed and, if so, how.

Retooling the Divided Self

Purpose

◆ To address a double bind, that is, a situation where one feels that, to be protected, one needs to do two contradictory actions.

Two-Minute Simple Balance

1. Drink water.

2. Hook up the hemispheres of the brain with *Heart Blessing.* With hands crossed over the chest, alternate tapping with each hand.

3. Rest in the heart for a moment with both hands on the heart.

Procedure

1. Hold one hand on the sacrum and one hand underneath the nose (GV 26) for two minutes. (This is the Space Button in Brain Gym.)

2. *Brain Flow Mudra:* Hold one hand on the back of the head and one hand on the forehead for two minutes.

3. Place one hand on the back of the head and one hand underneath the nose (GV26) for two minutes.

4. Place one hand on the back of the head and one hand on the sacrum for two minutes.

5. Place one hand under the collarbone (which corresponds to the thymus) and one hand on the heart for two minutes.

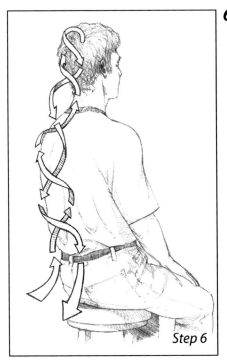

Step 6

6. *DNA Breath:* Breathe in from the sacrum, tracing a spiral with a breath to the crown, on the exhale breathing out an overlapping spiral, forming a life-giving double-helix DNA, creating a circular breath from the sacrum to the crown, and back down to the sacrum from the crown with the exhale. Do this for six breaths. It's helpful to say to self before beginning the visualization, "My DNA is continually evolving toward highest harmony."

Check-In

◆ Notice the sensations in your body. Notice if any feelings have changed and, if so, how.

Returning to the Heart

Purpose

- ◆ To work with addictive states by addressing the prefrontal cortex.
- ◆ To work with momentary situations where one is triggered or flooding.
- ◆ To respond to issues where procrastination is part of the pattern.

Two-Minute Simple Balance

1. Drink water.

2. Hook up the hemispheres of the brain with *Heart Blessing*. With hands crossed over the chest, alternate tapping with each hand.

3. Rest in the heart for a moment with both hands on the heart.

Procedure

1. *Basic Relief:* Hold one hand on the forehead and one hand beneath the nose (at GV26) for two minutes.

2. *Wise Brain Mudra:* Hold one hand on the crown and one hand on the forehead for two minutes.

Step 3

3. *Brain Flow Mudra:* Hold one hand on the back of the head and one hand on the forehead for two minutes.

Step 4

4. *Head-Heart Hold:* Hold one hand at the back of the head and one hand on the heart for two minutes.

Check-In

◆ Notice the sensations in your body. Notice if any feelings have changed and, if so, how.

Safe to Heal

Purpose

◆ To fluidly go back in time where there is heartache of any kind and respond now by sending to self the warmth and compassion that was needed then.

Two-Minute Simple Balance

1. Drink water.

2. Hook up the hemispheres of the brain with *Heart Blessing*. With hands crossed over the chest, alternate tapping with each hand.

3. Rest in the heart for a moment with both hands on the heart.

Procedure

1. *Double-Hands Heart Hold:* With both hands on the heart, think of yourself at a previous time where there remains an edge of hurt. Send loving kindness to the person that was you then, who needed comfort and care.

2. Hold one hand on the heart and one hand on the sacrum for two minutes.

3. Hold one hand on the sacrum and one hand on the chin for two minutes.

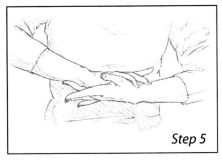

Step 5

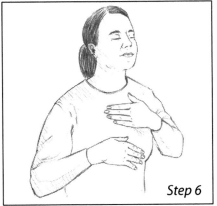

Step 6

4. Hold one hand on the sacrum and one hand on the crown for two minutes.

5. *Gate to Peace:* Fold your forearms in front of your chest, and then slide your arms out until your palms are on top of each other. Alternate tapping with the middle finger just below the wrist crease for about one minute. This provides bilateral stimulation of the brain while connecting with the pericardium meridian, which governs the heart.

6. *Heart Glide:* Glide one hand after another down over the heart to soothe the heart.

Check-In

◆ Notice the sensations in your body. Notice if any feelings have changed and, if so, how.

Self-Soothing in Troubled Times

Purpose

◆   To be in the present moment when there is much distress going on.

Two-Minute Simple Balance

1. Drink water.

2. Hook up the hemispheres of the brain with *Heart Blessing*. With hands crossed over the chest, alternate tapping with each hand.

3. Rest in the heart for a moment with both hands on the heart.

Procedure

1. Breathe in the difficult feelings. Breathe out, making the exhale longer than the inhale. Do this for 10 to 12 breaths.

2. *Green Means Go:* Imagine healing green light coming into the right hemisphere of your brain with the inhale, the green light picking up any trauma residue, traveling to the heart, continuing to pick up any trauma residue, and on the exhale going out your left leg and out the sole of your left foot. Do this five to 10 times.

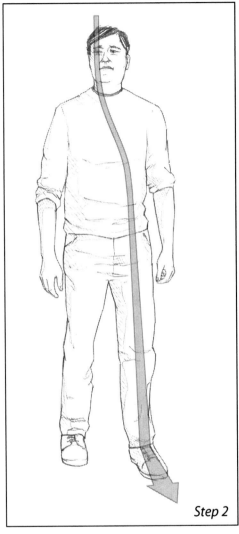

Step 2

3. *Eyelid Sweep:* With an index finger at the corner of each eye, gently pull the fingers over each eyelid, across the temple, and around the back of the earlobes. Then start over again. Do this 10 to 20 times.

4. Hold one hand on the heart and one hand two inches below the navel for two minutes. This gesture encourages a soft belly and an open heart.

5. Hold one hand below the navel and one hand on the sacrum for two minutes.

6. Hold one hand on the sacrum and one hand on the heart for two minutes.

7. Let your body soften. Let your body be. Settle into your body like you would settle into a comfy armchair after a long day.

Check-In

◆ Notice the sensations in your body. Notice if any feelings have changed and, if so, how.

Sexual Healing

Purpose

◆ To stay engaged with your erotic, creative self. Perhaps in our culture we all need sexual healing. This protocol acknowledges that need.

Two-Minute Simple Balance

1. Drink water.

2. Hook up the hemispheres of the brain with *Heart Blessing*. With hands crossed over the chest, alternate tapping with each hand.

3. Rest in the heart for a moment with both hands on the heart.

Procedure

Step 1

1. *Back Again:* Tap or hold the thymus (at the second rib on the sternum) with one hand while the other hand taps or holds the chin for two minutes.

2. Hold one hand below the navel and one hand on the heart for several minutes. This particular holding can be a powerful way to connect heart feelings to sexual feelings, as well as a gentle way to access feelings that may be interfering with sexual healing.

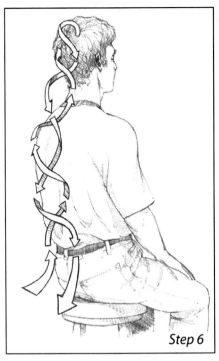

Step 6

3. Hold one hand below the navel and one hand at the back of the head for two minutes.

4. Hold one hand below the navel and one hand on the third eye for two minutes, visualizing your being as a fluid coherence of energy, like light sparkling on a body of water.

5. *Double-Hands Heart Hold:* Hold both hands on your heart, remembering your true, deep self.

6. *DNA Breath:* Breathe in from the sacrum, tracing a spiral with a breath to the crown, on the exhale breathing out an overlapping spiral, forming a life-giving double-helix DNA and creating a circular breath from the sacrum to the crown, and back down to the sacrum from the crown with the exhale. Do this for six breaths. It's helpful to say to self before beginning the visualization, "My DNA is continually evolving toward highest harmony."

7. Massage both earlobes, opening the senses.

Check-In

♦ Notice the sensations in your body. Notice if any feelings have changed and, if so, how.

Songs of the Heart

Purpose

- To address the limbic brain, that is, the deeply emotional part of our brain that attaches to others. It is the part of the brain that as a mammal is involved in taking care of our young in a nurturing way, that sings and plays, that dreams and carries the dream forward in relationships. The purpose of this protocol is to help grief wash through when there has been attachment and subsequent loss.

Two-Minute Simple Balance

1. Drink water.

2. Hook up the hemispheres of the brain with *Heart Blessing*. With hands crossed over the chest, alternate tapping with each hand.

3. Rest in the heart for a moment with both hands on the heart.

Procedure

1. *Head-Heart Hold:* With an intent to release grief, hold one hand on the back of the head and one hand on the heart for about two minutes. A basic belief is that we all carry old hurts and wounds that "fill" the heart. To name our grief and feel it in our body allows it to move through.

Step 1

2. *Forehead-Heart Hold:* With an intent to envision the heart's release, hold one hand on the forehead and one hand on the heart for about two minutes.

3. *Double-Hands Heart Hold:* With an intent to stabilize openness, hold both hands on the heart for about two minutes.

Step 4

4. *Synapse to Synapse:* With one hand, massage either side of the sternum at the collarbone (at K27) while the other hand is on the heart for two minutes.

5. *Gold-White Weave:* Imagine gold light going from the right hemisphere to the left hemisphere of your brain, at the same time imagining white light going from the left hemisphere to the right hemisphere, the golden white light overlapping, forming a radiant weave of light, filling the entire brain.

Check-In

◆ Notice the sensations in your body. Notice if any feelings have changed and, if so, how.

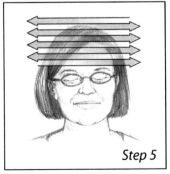

Step 5

Space That Holds All You Are

Purpose

◆ To make a place in the heart for all feelings, at the same time, to ease overwhelming feelings.

Two-Minute Simple Balance

1. Drink water.

2. Hook up the hemispheres of the brain with *Heart Blessing*. With hands crossed over the chest, alternate tapping with each hand.

3. Rest in the heart for a moment with both hands on the heart.

Procedure

1. Request that your heart's wisdom help you contain all the feelings of the situation, staying present in your body, connected and open to new understandings.

2. *Solid Ground:* With one hand, massage under the eyes (at St2) with the thumb and index finger with the other hand on the sacrum for two minutes.

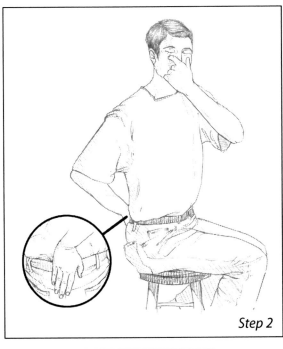

Step 2

3. Hold one hand on the sacrum and one hand on the heart for two minutes.

4. Tonglen is an ancient Tibetan Buddhist practice where, with the inhale, one brings in the pain of one's experience, with the exhale breathing out loving kindness and spaciousness. Breathe in the particular discomfort that is there now. Breathe out some manifestation of your basic goodness.

Step 5

5. *Spacious Heart Breath:* Breathe into the heart center and, with the breath, trace an infinity symbol (a sideways figure-8) and breathe out the heart center. Do this for six breaths.

Check-In

◆ Notice the sensations in your body. Notice if any feelings have changed and, if so, how.

Speaking One's Truth

Purpose

◆ To access one's deeper knowing and speak from that place.

Two-Minute Simple Balance

1. Drink water.

2. Hook up the hemispheres of the brain with *Heart Blessing*. With hands crossed over the chest, alternate tapping with each hand.

3. Rest in the heart for a moment with both hands on the heart.

Procedure

1. *Laser Like:* Do *Wise Brain Mudra* (one hand on the forehead, one hand on the crown) for one minute followed by *Brain Flow Mudra* (one hand on the forehead, one hand on the back of the head) for two minutes.

2. Hold one hand on the throat and one hand on the crown for two minutes.

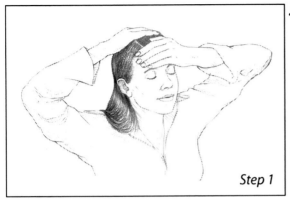

Step 1

3. Hold one hand on the throat and one hand on the heart for two minutes. This is a gesture that represents speaking from the heart.

4. Hold one hand on the throat and one hand on the solar plexus (midway between the navel and the base of the sternum) for two minutes.

Step 1

5. Find three truths your heart wants you to know, perhaps a prayer that is just waiting to be heard.

6. Read these sentences to yourself or say them aloud: May I speak my truth. May we all live in truth.

Check-In

◆ Notice the sensations in your body. Notice if any feelings have changed and, if so, how.

Sun and the Moon First Aid

Purpose

◆ To relieve distress and accompanying emotions.

Two-Minute Simple Balance

1. Drink water.

2. Hook up the hemispheres of the brain with *Heart Blessing*. With hands crossed over the chest, alternate tapping with each hand.

3. Rest in the heart for a moment with both hands on the heart.

Procedure

Step 1

1. *Back Again:* Tap or hold the thymus (at the second rib on the sternum) while at the same time tapping or holding the chin for two minutes.

2. Hold one hand below the navel and one hand on the forehead at the third eye while visualizing a golden moon at the third eye.

3. Hold one hand below the navel and one hand at the solar plexus (midway between the navel and the base of the sternum), visualizing a vibrant sun at the solar plexus.

Step 5

4. *Brain Flow Mudra:* Hold one hand on the back of the head and one hand on the forehead for two minutes, with the intention to convert distress into creativity.

5. *Head-Heart Hold:* Hold one hand on the back of the head and one hand on the heart for two minutes.

Check-In

◆ Notice the sensations in your body. Notice if any feelings have changed and, if so, how.

Note

◆ It is helpful to take a quick assessment of your level of distress before and after doing this protocol. Use a 1 to 10 scale, with 10 being high distress and 1 feeling peaceful. If, after doing the protocol once, your distress is 4 or higher on the scale, it is helpful to do another round of the protocol for the remaining distress.

Three-Step Flow

Purpose

◆ To soothe.

◆ To harmonize body energy when there is arousal.

◆ To set an intention in the mind and body.

◆ To access feelings in a state where feelings are not readily available.

Two-Minute Simple Balance

1. Drink water.

2. Hook up the hemispheres of the brain with *Heart Blessing.* With hands crossed over the chest, alternate tapping with each hand.

3. Rest in the heart for a moment with both hands on the heart.

Procedure

Step 1

1. *Brain Flow Mudra:* Hold one hand on the back of the head and one hand on the forehead for two minutes.

2. *Head-Heart Hold:* Hold one hand on the back of the head and one hand on the heart for two minutes.

Step 2

3. *Double-Hands Heart Hold:* Hold both hands on the heart for two minutes.

Check-In

♦ Notice the sensations in your body. Notice if any feelings have changed and, if so, how.

Note

♦ For couples, one person does the holding for the partner. On the third step, the partner places one hand on the person's back in the area of the heart and one hand on the heart.

Voice and Vision

Purpose

♦ To give voice; to give expression to one's dreams.

♦ To speak with truth and power about one's experience of the world.

Two-Minute Simple Balance

1. Drink water.

2. Hook up the hemispheres of the brain with *Heart Blessing*. With hands crossed over the chest, alternate tapping with each hand.

3. Rest in the heart for a moment with both hands on the heart.

Procedure

1. Place one hand on the throat (fifth chakra) and one hand on the heart (fourth chakra) for two minutes.

2. Place one hand on the throat (fifth chakra) and one hand on the third eye (sixth chakra) for two minutes.

3. Place one hand on the throat (fifth chakra) and one hand below the navel (second chakra) for two minutes.

4. Place one hand on the throat (fifth chakra) and one hand on the solar plexus (third chakra) for two minutes.

Check-In

◆ Notice the sensations in your body. Notice if any feelings have changed and, if so, how.

Wake Up

Purpose

♦ To disrupt a trance state where there is a feeling of being on automatic with a dysfunctional pattern.

Two-Minute Simple Balance

1. Drink water.

2. Hook up the hemispheres of the brain with *Heart Blessing*. With hands crossed over the chest, alternate tapping with each hand.

3. Rest in the heart for a moment with both hands on the heart.

Procedure

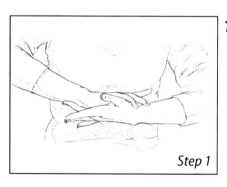

Step 1

1. *Gate to Peace:* Fold your forearms in front of your chest, and then slide your arms out until your palms are on top of each other. Alternate tapping with the middle finger just below the wrist crease for about one minute. This provides bilateral stimulation of the brain while connecting with the pericardium meridian, which governs the heart.

Step 2

2. *Back Again:* Tap or hold the thymus (at the second rib on the sternum) while also tapping or holding the chin for two minutes.

3. Hold one hand on the solar plexus, midway between the navel and the base of the sternum, and one hand on the forehead at the third eye for two minutes.

Step 4

4. *Basic Relief:* Hold one hand on the forehead and one hand beneath the nose (at GV26) for two minutes.

5. *Eye Opener:* Make a sideways figure-8 eye movement (eyes upper right, lower right, upper left, lower left, and back to upper right) while holding hands on the heart for two minutes.

Step 5

6. Shake your hands out.

Check-In

♦ Notice the sensations in your body. Notice if any feelings have changed and, if so, how.

When the World is Too Much

Purpose

◆ To facilitate peace, keep breathing, and stay in the body. This protocol is a useful tool to help regulate emotional flooding.

Two-Minute Simple Balance

1. Drink water.

2. Hook up the hemispheres of the brain with *Heart Blessing.* With hands crossed over the chest, alternate tapping with each hand.

3. Rest in the heart for a moment with both hands on the heart.

Procedure

1. *Green Means Go:* Imagine healing green light coming into the right hemisphere of your brain with the inhale, the green light picking up any trauma residue, traveling to the heart, continuing to pick up any trauma residue, and on the exhale going down your left leg and out the sole of your left foot. Do this for two minutes.

2. *Synapse to Synapse:* With one hand, massage either side of the sternum at the collarbone (at K27) while the other hand is on the heart for two minutes.

Step 2

3. Hold one hand on the heart and one hand on the sacrum for two minutes.

4. Hold one hand on the sacrum and one hand two inches below the navel for two minutes.

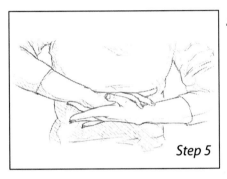
Step 5

5. *Gate to Peace:* Fold your forearms in front of your chest, and then slide your arms out until your palms are on top of each other. Alternate tapping with the middle finger just below the wrist crease for about one minute. This provides bilateral stimulation of the brain while connecting with the pericardium meridian, which governs the heart.

Check-In

◆ Notice the sensations in your body. Notice if any feelings have changed and, if so, how.

Part IV.

Addendum

for Clinicians

8.

Using Energy Protocols in Psychotherapy

Therapy is essentially about healing the heart. An individual comes to therapy because the heart is hurting, perhaps closed in a way that interferes with a basic well-being. Whatever the particular stories a client brings to the therapy, somewhere, somehow, a trust has been broken. We are trained in developing a therapeutic alliance to help bring forward the sense of self that has been injured, so that repair may happen. The work is of course both internal and relational, intrapersonal and interpersonal. The issues may involve trauma residue syndrome or post-traumatic stress disorder. In either case, providing resource, so the client can connect to the body, and feel with the heart.

Trauma and hardship can be like static on the radio interfering with an open listening to the body's signals. Many of the protocols are designed to lower heightened levels of arousal while the client is working through and as a result help the client regulate trauma states both in session and out of session. This helps remove the static, so the body can return to a clear, bright perception and a grounded awareness with the senses.

It is the body that takes the harm—emotionally or physically—and it is the body that recovers the ability to be present with a loving attention. The protocols were developed in a clinical setting to work with clinical issues and they stand on their own. They provide the possibility to deepen one's relationship to self by increasing confidence that one can negotiate intense feeling states in a short period of time with the end result being greater physical well-being and coherence.

So often, when there is a history of trauma, there is also a history of going away from the body with dissociative states, with self harm, with various addictive states. These protocols are created as a gentle way to return to the body, going away from the body, and returning again and again. Doing this, a new pattern comes into existence, one that supports the body as it learns how to soothe in the midst of disrupting the negative neurological feedback loop. For example, the protocol *Beginning Again* is useful to clients with early unresolved attachment issues.

I believe that there is not yet a full reckoning with the extent that trauma symptoms become somatically wired in the body. These protocols are about releasing the stored sensations of experience, so that the body's wisdom and insight can come forward.

The model I am proposing is transmuting trauma with a paradigm shift in percentages: forty percent of the work is directly with the suffering and sixty percent is about stabilizing the resources, thereby furthering energetic cohesion and trauma resolution. Here we have a place of supporting the client by going into the shadow to bring forward the unresolved pain and supporting the client flourishing in their life.

The energy for the flourishing is claimed every time a person journeys into the underworld of their wounding and comes back with greater intactness, and less identification with the trauma state. This becomes a definition of empowerment: going into the dark hurt places, feeling, feeling, and getting out of the trauma state changed with more resource at hand.

This model of transmuting trauma is about pulsing back and forth between old ways of protecting and new ways of growth; pulsing back and forth between previously held intolerable feelings and feeling open in the moment; pulsing back and forth between charged trauma material and a curiosity about what is underneath; pulsing back and forth between an aversion to a core self that feels damaged to a deeper resonance with a true self under the distress. This is an experience of a state of being where nothing is disavowed. Inherent in this model is increasing body coherency with negative emotions by quickening the working through process, the recovery period from strong emotions.

I am defining empowerment as a place where survival issues are triggered and there remains a willingness to be present. A place of higher brain function informed by the heart. This has no context unless there is great appreciation for what it takes to go against previous conditioning. Adaptive responses get wired in early on because of necessity. If the perceived threat to well being is large enough, the adaptive response gets paired with a felt experience of threat in regards to survival. This means the person feels like they're going to die unless they adapt, because the caretaker in the environment is either out of control or absent. It is that straightforward.

The adaptive response is in fact no choice because if they don't adapt the person believes they will not make it. Therefore, to look at changing old coping mechanisms can bring up extreme anxiety. The gain that occurs over time is in accessing what I am calling the fundamental core belief. It is the wholeness underneath the trauma that states: As I stand in my truth, I have resource, coherence, and presence. A hard-earned place that is achieved only by repeatedly challenging the identification with the trauma state and the coping mechanisms that developed from it.

The skills needed to deal with trauma residue are similar to those needed to be fully present with the terror of healthy, deep attachment, and vulnerability. So, we get to undo the prohibition about being in the body, returning again and again to the body, the feeling in the body, the presence of the body.

The question becomes how to do this in a therapeutic setting, how to keep the frame of a clinical hour and work mind/body issues, furthering body integration without touch. I offer some guideposts along the path:

1. The golden rule in therapy as a therapist seems to be about doing one's own work. What that means in this case is being

familiar with how feelings manifest in the body with one's own experience with hardship.

2. Be a work in progress. It is helpful of course to have familiarity with the protocols, one's own body experience, and from that vantage point suggest them in a clinical hour. Everyone's confidence increases when there is a decrease on the SUDs marking (subjective units of distress scale). Simply, it is asking clients on a scale of 0 to 10, with 10 being high distress and 0 being no distress, where they are before and after doing a protocol.

3. Guide the protocol by naming what to do, timing it, and having a parallel process of doing the protocol for oneself at the same time the client is doing it. For many clients this helps them to feel supported, joined with in a healthy way, rather than observed. The exception is whenever there is a sideways figure-8 movement. At these places, lead the eye movement by having the client watch your index and middle finger as you make a sideways figure-8 in front of them beginning at the center point and going upper right, lower right, upper left, lower left. A benefit for the therapist doing the protocol with the client within the hour is that it is revitalizing to both. Trauma work becomes less draining, less overwhelming. Both parties get to return to the body, balancing body chemistry.

4. Let the protocol stand on its own by processing what happened during the protocol after the SUDs rating is taken. If there is a strong expression of feeling during a protocol, it is most probably about movement through a feeling. The protocol holds the frame. The clinician's job is to be there when the protocol is completed and hear the client's feelings and insights and relate them to the beginning of an hour.

5. A protocol is particularly helpful when the client is working with charged material and there is high arousal, or in the same situation and there is a flat affect. The protocols seem to help the nervous system metabolize and regulate body states. For many clients, this is about working with core material and

maintaining body coherence at the same time.

6. The protocols provide an avenue to unlock traumatic conditioning. The key to quickening the healing with this kind of body-integrated psychotherapy is stability and safety. The protocols are designed with both in mind.

7. When there has been abuse in a client's history, there will more likely than not be a distrust of feelings, of perception, of the body. The client using the protocols in a session gets to experience that if the body lets down a bit from habitual defenses, there can be an experience of surprising relief, and repeated over time this is a vehicle to regain confidence in the body's resiliency and resource. This furthers all aspects of the therapy.

8. The success of the therapy hour of course is about how the person can manifest the goodness of the working-through in his or her day-to-day life. The protocols help to maintain the holding environment of therapy in regular life. They are soothing and comforting. They work. And they are infinitely adaptable. Individual gestures of a protocol can be done in a grocery store or in the shower. Wherever. It is not vital to do all of the protocol exactly. It *is* vital to learn new means of self-regulating. Trust clients' spontaneous adaptations. They know what their bodies need.

9. The protocols are designed to help people discover and read their body signals. For this to happen, the static needs to be cleared. Once this is done the person gets to explore for instance how excitement feels similar and different from anxiety in the body.

10. There can be a tremendous pain in healing the body/mind/spirit. With that, there can be a grace in allowing the unfolding of an inherent vitality and instinct that will be kept down no longer.

I believe that using energy protocols within a therapeutic hour is not just cutting edge, but also a clinical necessity for working with clients with whom there has been severe trauma. Trauma work is a long haul. Energy protocols are a way as a clinician to lighten the way, include the body, and stabilize the change.

The difficulty for many of us isn't about willingness, but rather how to integrate traditional psychotherapy with body-focused protocols. Where are the models that show us how to do both, rather than have it be either talk therapy or body work in a therapeutic setting? My sense is that the paradigm shift that is at the threshold of manifesting collectively is about negotiating in a therapy hour, head and heart, heart and body. Practically speaking, that means we get to learn how to fluidly go from listening, exploring, and making interpretations to helping the client notice body states and work with them, and back again to verbally understand what has just happened. This helps a client move between the limbic brain and the right hemisphere, to the left the hemisphere, making a cohesive narrative in the process of going back and forth between thinking and feeling.

We are divided into two camps: those who primarily use verbal insight and expression as the modality to healing and those who are body focused. Maybe it is time to weave together the best of both.

For me, Eugene Gendlin with his book *Focusing* was a pioneer in moving us toward looking at a holistic body sense, a "felt sense." His book was printed in 1978. Many splendid techniques and schools have evolved over the years. To name a few: Hakomi therapy, EMDR, Process Work with Arnie Mindell, and in 2000 Babette Rothchild's book *The Body Remembers*. Good stuff. Let our training be about bringing us back to the body, so that what happens in a therapy hour is about a felt shift. Clients get to take with them the internalized therapeutic relationship that helps them be in their body, embodied, ready to meet the world.

On another note, I believe as a therapeutic community we are critically under-resourced in ways to help facilitate affect tolerance with positive regard. We work with the distress, help the client hold the distress, and then often neglect to help the client hold the satisfactions and gains in life. This is both about receiving praise as well as an internal place of esteem after a job well done. As therapists, we have the privilege of providing a frame, and we help hold the honoring of self that the client gets to do. This open-heartedness is such a precious experience and is as delicate as a mountain meadow.

As human beings, as adults healing, we get to be vulnerable to the extent that we are empowered. Our vulnerability is usually a match for our power and strength. They go hand in hand. What this means in a clinical hour is that the client gets to experience a disregulated affect state, and in the same hour the ability to work with the arousal, self-soothe, be in the body, and leave feeling intact. This generates enormous confidence over time. For many clients, this newfound place is about trusting the feeling body and the ability to negotiate whatever comes up.

Part of the sense of protection with regard to the vulnerability comes from opening the perceptual field. Trauma experience closes the aperture on what is consciously felt, which usually results in a very narrow band of perception. This is survival mode. The continued difficulty is that often the lens through which the person sees the world at the time of trauma gets locked into position. As the nervous system begins to unlock and the trauma gets metabolized, a full sensory perception becomes available. This is power. Power to make choices based on body signals that further a solid sense of self.

I believe we are at a threshold with how as a community we have been doing trauma work. The vision being brought forward looks like this to me: a body-oriented psychotherapy that is relational and process oriented. The work of course addresses trauma issues and beliefs in the ways we have been trained. At the same time, the work has a dynamic flow between metabolizing background shame with body-based interventions and helping clients to bring their stories, their dreams forward to the present moment. It is interesting to note that happiness is one of the predictors of cohesion.

Shame is like a sticky glue that holds things together. It is often so pervasive that it is difficult to recognize that it is there at all. Generally, as clinicians, we have not been trained to "see" it. Instead, we deal with the repercussions of shame rather than going to the root cause. Imagine if we don't see the shame how challenging it is for the client to see what is most disowned in them. Shame shuts down the naming of other feelings and the ability to release them. This feeling place of unworthiness is probably not accessible to conscious experience. Naming and working the shame, for example with a protocol, reduces the shame. The resulting intactness instills a sense of worthiness.

The client in trauma work discovers that bringing forward the split off wounded places, such as shame, is in many ways like a traditional shamanic soul retrieval, giving access to a true self place that predates the harm. Defenses are often too effective. They keep out the traumatic incidents as well as the remembering of the larger self. I don't believe that there needs to be a careful mapping of memories. My experience is that what does need to be processed are the places of tonic immobility or hyperarousal, and the defensive patterns that are connected to these places. As one of my mentors has said, "You don't need to dig up the past. You can trip over it in the present." A client brings to the session upset from everyday life and the question becomes, "What is that experience like in your body?" Once a person is truly in their body, often with the help of energy work, their own insights and understandings will unfold. The body states from the trauma get unlocked from the nervous system, metabolized, and the true self is brought forward, able to discern in most circumstances what is old material and what is happening in the present moment.

Sometimes with the protocols clients are frustrated that they don't eliminate feelings. In fact, the protocols can bring new feelings up. Being in the feeling body at this point is like being on a bike with training wheels. The choice becomes about comfort or coherence. Or rather, how to negotiate the experience of being in the feeling body with moderate levels of discomfort while coherence is gained. There is the paradox we all know about going into material with a client, and at the end of the hour the client is relieved to have worked through dreaded material.

The clinical commitment can be to support the client reclaiming the feeling body, and the assurance that energy work can be done at the end of the hour if needed, so the client leaves with a feeling of cohesion. It is interesting to note that energy work, protocols, can be used to explore territory as well as to initiate a sense of peacefulness. In part, it is the intent that one begins with. For example, if shame is released, it is probable there will be other feelings underneath the inhibitory aegis of shame. As a general rule of thumb, energy work seems to balance the nervous system. This helps to give the biochemical foundation for opening safely to the relational work within the therapeutic dyad.

There is a window of opportunity within the clinical hour where any energy gesture will be extremely potent, and that is when the client is agitated or disassociated. When there has been trauma and the person is in the here and now and in distress, it seems to provide direct access biochemically to previous upsetting body states. A healing physical gesture to the body, like *Head-Heart Hold,* quickens the work. This is not a cognitive recognition reaching back. This is a body state coming forward to be integrated in the present moment. This is about providing the frame so the client can hold the body experience and thus achieve more body cohesion. This facilitates relationship within the therapeutic relationship and relationship in the rest of the individual's life. The confidence to have a felt body experience is the ground of our being. From this place, we venture out to explore the world.

Much of our memory is implicit memory, which is the emotional memory present at birth and involves the amygdala, in contrast to explicit memory which develops from the second year of life, and involves the hippocampus and is autobiographical. Energy work can key into implicit memory and the feelings that are trapped in our cells that the nervous system is responding to by endlessly repeating. I believe this is the origination of psychological patterns that we all play out in a myriad of ways. The body has an experience and if it is an intense one, and there is no safe way at the time for there to be full release, then all or part of it gets tucked away. We may have a narrative (explicit memory) about it or we may not. Traditionally, psychotherapy aims for the narrative. It is of great benefit of course to give words to our stories. The difficulty is taking this for the whole thing. The body understands more than it is able to give words to. Gestures that key into the body's energetic circuitry may communicate in a way that words cannot.

My favorite definition of therapy is Rowe Mortimer's:

Therapy is the process of attending to someone while they enact or tell their story with the hope that they will be able to over time accomplish the following:

1. As more of the story is told and thought and experienced, they will be less obliged to act it out and more free to live life in a contemporarily rewarding way;

2. They will need to leave less and less of the story out, either in terms of thoughts or powerful feelings;

3. Their story will increase in richness and continuity and sense;

4. The story will be told with an increasingly sympathetic understanding of self and of the rest of the cast of characters.

I would like to be so bold as to make an addition:

5. The individual has increased connection and awareness of body states across time.

There is currently a resurgence of interest in attachment theory, in particular attachment theory that joins with state-of-the-art brain research. We now get to talk about limbic regulation, the brain and intimacy, and how physiology interfaces with our ability to relate. Relationships, matters of the heart, are the core of human existence. Trauma, as we know, interrupts "going on being," trauma patterns ensue, and the bottom line is that our ability to relate in a heartfelt way is compromised.

This extends to the activation of trauma patterns that occur interpersonally. Alan Schore talks about the loss of the ability to regulate the intensity of feelings being the most comprehensive lingering effect of early trauma and neglect, which brings us back to the protocols and the affect regulation they provide. By connecting the mind/body interface of trauma states, the ability for healthy attachment increases.

A person in the midst of core material responds in a fresh way after doing energy work. The trauma pattern gets reworked, renegotiated by the very act of a person self-soothing in a way that benefits when there is great upset. This gives the person the opportunity to be in the feeling body without being overwhelmed or disconnected, furthering mindfulness and loving kindness.

The outline of the clinical goals of the protocols is as follows:

1. The protocols provide containment by easing excessive stimulation, lessening defensive numbing, and helping to avoid emotional collapse.

2. The protocols, energy work in general, bilateral stimulation of the brain, all seem to access implicit memory.

3. The protocols take the charge off of a memory or an intense emotional state such as shame in order to be with the feeling underneath. This changes the clinical hour by allowing the client to safely go deeply into strong body states and back out again to an "everyday" self in a 50-minute hour.

4. The protocols generate an intactness of self by giving a structure to metabolize feelings and return to a larger self, thereby increasing resiliency, insight, and wisdom.

5. The protocols provide a biochemical means to stabilize regard towards self. Without sustained intent to integrate esteem, the backlash of the old conditioning can be terrible.

6. The protocols establish body coherence as a biological marker of working through. Past, present, and future are all on board: metabolizing trauma patterns, being in the body in the present moment, and confidence that one can realize one's dreams.

This book is my attempt to negotiate through the straits of psychodynamic theory, trauma theory, attachment theory, current brain research, energy work, and maintain a relational context within the clinical hour. The struggle and synthesis are an ongoing process. What never leaves is my belief that regard for self and healthy attachment to others is the be-all and end-all, and by increasing the capacity for complexity and range of affect, both are furthered. When it is safe to be in the body, openness and curiosity awaken, and healthy attachment gets to grow deep roots. With loving connection to other, an individual's worthiness knows no limit.

Related Resources

Amen, Daniel. *Change Your Brain, Change Your Life.* New York: Three Rivers Press, 1998.

Benson, Herbert. *The Relaxation Response.* New York: Avon Books: 1974.

Bregman Ehrenberg, Darlene. *The Intimate Edge.* New York: W.W. Norton & Company, 1992.

Bromberg, Phillip. *Standing in the Spaces.* Hillsdale, NJ: The Analytic Press, 1998.

Chidre, Doc; Martin, Howard. *The Heartmath Solution.* San Francisco: Harper Press: 1999.

Cohen, Kenneth. *The Way of Qigong.* New York: Ballantine Publishing Group, 1997.

Cozolino, Louis. *The Neuroscience of Psychotherapy.* New York: W. W. Norton & Company, 2002.

Dalai Lama; Cutler, Howard. *The Art of Happiness at Work.* New York: Riverhead Books, 2003.

Dennison, Paul; Dennison, Gail. *Brain Gym.* Ventura, CA: Edu-Kinesthetics, 1989.

Diamond, John. *Your Body Doesn't Lie.* New York: Harper & Row, 1979.

Dossey, Larry. *Reinventing Medicine.* San Francisco: Harper, 1999.

Eden, Donna. *Energy Medicine.* New York: Penguin Putnam, 1998.

Gach, Michael Reed. *Acupressure's Potent Points.* New York: Bantam Books, 1990.

Gendlin, Eugene. *Focusing.* New York: Everest House, 1978.

Gerber, Richard. *Vibrational Medicine.* Rochester, Vermont: Bear & Company, 2001.

Goleman, Daniel. *Destructive Emotions: A Scientific Dialogue with the Dalai Lama.* New York: Bantam Books, 2004.

Judith, Anodea. *Wheels of Life.* St Paul, MN: Llewellyn Publications, 1999.

Kapchuk, Ted. *The Web That Has No Weaver: Understanding Chinese Medicine.* New York: McGraw-Hill, 2000.

Levine, Peter. *Waking the Tiger: Healing Trauma.* Berkeley, CA: North Atlantic Books, 1997.

Lewis, Thomas; Amini, Fairi; Lannon, Richard. *A General Theory Of Love.* New York: Vintage Books, 2001.

Lipton, Bruce. *The Biology of Belief.* Santa Rosa, CA: Elite Books, 2005.

Lowen, Alexander. *Bioenergetics.* New York: Penguin Books, 1975.

Mindell, Arnold. *Quantum Mind.* Portland, Oregon: Lao Tse Press, 2000.

Moyers, Bill. *Healing and the Mind.* New York: Double Day, 1993.

Ornstein, Robert; Sobel, David. *The Healing Brain.* New York: Touchstone Books, 1987.

Pert, Candace. *Molecules of Emotion.* New York: Touchstone Books, 1997.

Prigogine, Ilya. *Order Out of Chaos.* New York: Bantam Books, 1984.

Promislow, Sharon. *Putting Out the Fire of Fear.* West Vancouver, BC: Enhanced Learning & Integration, 2002.

Rothschild, Babette. *The Body Remembers: The Psychophysiology of Trauma and Trauma Treatment.* New York: W.W. Norton & Company, 2000.

Schore, Allan. *Affect Regulation and the Origin of the Self.* Hillsdale, NJ: Lawrence Erlbaum, 1994.

Siegel, Daniel. *The Developing Mind.* New York: Guilford Press, 1999.

So, James. *The Book of Acupuncture Points.* Brookline, MA: Paradigm Publications, 1985.

Thie, John. *Touch For Health.* Sherman Oaks, CA: T.H. Enterprises, 1994.

van der Kolk, Bessel; McFarlane, Alexander; Weisaeth, Lars. *Traumatic Stress: The Effects of Overwhelming Experience on Mind, Body, and Society.* New York: Guilford Press, 1996.

Index

Printed in the United States
122288LV00005B/269/P

9 780979 510106